40-Day Journey with Kathleen Norris

Other books in the

40-DAY *Journey*
Series

40-Day Journey with Joan Chittister
Beverly Lanzetta, Editor

40-Day Journey with Dietrich Bonhoeffer
Ron Klug, Editor

40-Day Journey with Martin Luther
Gracia M. Grindal, Editor

40-DAY
Journey

WITH KATHLEEN NORRIS

40-Day Journey Series

Kathryn Haueisen, Editor

Augsburg Books

Minneapolis

40-DAY JOURNEY WITH KATHLEEN NORRIS

Cover design: Laurie Ingram
Cover photo: Gregory Yamamoto

Library of Congress Cataloging-in-Publication Data
Norris, Kathleen, 1947-
40-day journey with Kathleen Norris / Kathryn Haueisen, editor.
    p. cm. — (40-day journey series)
Includes bibliographical references.
ISBN 978-0-8066-8040-8 (alk. paper)
1. Spirituality. 2. Spiritual life—Christianity. 3. Devotional
exercises. I. Haueisen, Kathy. II. Title. III. Title: Forty day journey
with Kathleen Norris.
BV4501.3.N663 2008
242'.2—dc22
        2007042395

Printed in Canada.

12   11   10   09   3   4   5   6   7   8

CONTENTS

Series Introduction   7

Preface   9

How to Use this Book   11

Hints on Keeping a Journal   15

Who Is Kathleen Norris?   17

Journey Day 1-40   22

Journey's End   103

For Further Reading   104

Sources   105

SERIES INTRODUCTION

Imagine spending forty days with a great spiritual guide who has both the wisdom and the experience to help you along the path of your own spiritual journey. Imagine being able to listen to and question spiritual guides from the past and the present. Imagine being, as it were, mentored by women and men who have made their own spiritual journey and have recorded the landmarks, detours, bumps in the road, potholes, and wayside rests that they encountered along the way—all to help others (like you) who must make their own journey.

The various volumes in Augsburg Books' *40-Day Journey Series* are all designed to do just that—to lead you where your mind and heart and spirit long to go. As Augustine once wrote: *"You have made us for yourself, O Lord, and our heart is restless until it rests in you."* The wisdom you will find in the pages of this series of books will give you the spiritual tools and direction to find that rest. But there is nothing quietistic in the spirituality you will find here. Those who would guide you on this journey have learned that the heart that rests in God is one that lives with deeper awareness, deeper creativity, deeper energy, and deeper passion and commitment to the things that matter to God.

An ancient Chinese proverb states the obvious: the journey of a thousand miles begins with the first step. In a deep sense, books in the *40-Day Journey Series* are first steps on a journey that will not end when the forty days are over. No one can take the first step (or any step) for you.

Imagine that you are on the banks of the Colorado River. You are here to go white-water rafting for the first time and your guide has just described the experience, telling you with graphic detail what to expect. It sounds both exciting and frightening. You long for the experience but are somewhat disturbed, anxious, and uncertain in the face of the danger that promises to accompany you on the journey down the river. The guide gets into the raft.

She will accompany you on the journey, but she can't take the journey for you. If you want to experience the wildness of the river, the raw beauty of the canyon, the camaraderie of adventurers, and the mystery of a certain oneness with nature (and nature's creator), then you've got to get in the boat.

This book in your hand is like that. It describes the journey, provides a "raft," and invites you to get in. Along with readings from your spiritual guide, you will find scripture to mediate on, questions to ponder, suggestions for personal journaling, guidance in prayer, and a prayer for the day. If done faithfully each day, you will find the wisdom and encouragement you need to integrate meaningful spiritual insights and practices into your daily life. And when the 40-day journey is over it no longer will be the guide's description of the journey that stirs your longing for God but *your own experience* of the journey that grounds your faith and life and keeps you on the path.

I would encourage you to pick up other books in the series. There is only one destination, but many ways to get there. Not everything in every book will work for you (we are all unique), but in every book you will find much to help you discover your own path on the journey to the One in whom we all "live and move and have our being" (Acts 17:28).

May all be well with you on the journey.
Henry F. French, Series Editor

PREFACE

Kathleen Norris was born in Washington, D.C., and raised in Virginia and Illinois. She spent many childhood summers at her grandparents' home in Lemmon, South Dakota, until her family moved to Hawaii when she was eleven. After graduating from Bennington College in Vermont, she settled into the writing community of New York City. There she began her career as a poet, along with her late husband, David Dwyer, also a poet.

Some also consider her a prophet. I consider her an architect—an architect with words. Her words build powerful images of life, love, hope, grief, faith, peace, and spiritual growth within community. Much of her writing has been formed by her experiences as an oblate in the Benedictine community and the many years she and her late husband lived in her grandmother's home in South Dakota. Her profound insights about faith and life have been fueled as much by her absence from the faith community of her childhood as her return to it after twenty years away.

In addition to being a poet, Kathleen Norris is also a preacher and a student of early church theologians and monastics. She frequently has shared her love of words with school children as a guest teacher. She is a published author many times over. But most importantly for our 40-day journey with her, she is an architect who uses words to describe the ways our human joys and sorrows connect with the divine author of life.

Within the Benedictine community she has heard the word of God through the discipline of the daily office. She also has taken time to absorb the word through long periods of silence and solitude. Her words speak eloquently of the word who became flesh and dwelt among us.

One of the things I treasure about her writing is the research she does on the root meaning of words. For example, she explains that the word "salvation" literally means "to make wide" or "to make sufficient." She encourages her readers to discover how God is working "to make wide," or "to make sufficient" the path they are taking.

Based on her studies of the writings of Gregory of Nyssa, a fourth-century theologian, she teaches that sin is the refusal to grow. We get stuck in immaturity, repeating the same counterproductive and sometimes harmful behaviors over and over because we do not mature into the word of God and the transforming power of Christ.

She explains that the word we translate as perfect (as in, "Be perfect, therefore, as your heavenly Father is perfect," Matthew 5:48) does *not* mean to achieve the impossible goal of being error free. It comes from a Latin word that means complete or full grown and is an invitation to spiritual maturity.

She openly describes her own fears and failures of faith in ways that invite us to explore ours so we may put them aside and believe again. Yet while her writings give us an amazingly open and personal glimpse of her own thoughts and experiences, she also writes eloquently about the centrality of community. She understands in a very deep way that we all are impacted by the people around us, even when they are present only in our memories.

Kathy Haueisen

How to Use this Book

Your 40-day journey with Kathleen Norris gives you the opportunity to be mentored by a great contemporary spiritual writer and Christian leader. The purpose of the journey, however, is not just to gain "head knowledge" about Kathleen Norris. Rather, it is to begin living what you learn.

You will probably benefit most by fixing a special time of day in which to "meet with" your spiritual mentor. It is easier to maintain a spiritual practice if you do it regularly at the same time. For many people mornings, while the house is still quiet and before the busyness of the day begins, is a good time. Others will find that the noon hour or before bedtime serves well. We are all unique. Some of us are "morning people" and some of us are not. Do whatever works *for you* to maintain a regular meeting with Kathleen Norris. Write it into your calendar and do your best to keep your appointments.

It is best if you complete your 40-day journey in forty days. A deepening focus and intensity of experience will be the result. However, it is certainly better to complete the journey than to give it up because you can't get it done in forty days. Indeed, making it a 40- or 20-week journey may better fit your schedule and it just might be that spending a whole week, or perhaps half a week, reflecting on the reading, the scripture, and the prayers, and then practicing what you are learning could be a powerfully transforming experience as well. Again, set a schedule that works for you, only be consistent.

Each day of the journey begins with a reading from Kathleen Norris. You will note that the readings, from day to day, build on each other and introduce you to key ideas in her understanding of Christian life and faith. Read each selection slowly, letting the words sink into your consciousness. You may want to read each selection two or three times before moving on, perhaps reading it out loud once.

Following the reading from Kathleen Norris's writings, you will find the heading *Biblical Wisdom* and a brief passage from the Bible that relates directly to what she has said. As with the selection from Kathleen, read the biblical text slowly, letting the words sink into your consciousness.

Following the biblical reading, you will find the heading *Silence for Meditation.* Here you should take anywhere from five to twenty minutes meditating on the two readings. Begin by getting centered. Sit with your back straight, eyes closed, hands folded in your lap, and breathe slowly and deeply. Remember that breath is a gift of God; it is God's gift of life. Do nothing for two or three minutes other than simply observe your breath. Focus your awareness on the end of your nose. Feel the breath enter through your nostrils and leave through your nostrils.

Once you feel your mind and spirit settling down, open your eyes and read both the daily reading and the biblical text again. Read them slowly, focus on each word or phrase, savor them, explore possible meanings and implications. At the end of each day you will find a blank page with the heading *Notes.* As you meditate on the readings, jot down any insights that occur to you. Do the readings raise any questions for you? Write them down. Do the readings suggest anything you should do? Write it down.

Stay at it as long as it feels useful. When your mind is ready to move on, close your eyes and observe your breath for a minute or so. Then return to the book and the next heading: *Questions to Ponder.* Here you will find a few pointed questions by Kathy Haueisen, the book's compiler and editor, on the day's reading. These are general questions intended for all spiritual seekers and communities of faith. Think them through and write your answers (and the implications of your answers for your own life of faith and for your community of faith) in the *Notes* section.

Many of these *Questions to Ponder* are designed to remind us that although spirituality is always personal, it is simultaneously relational and communal. A number of the questions, therefore, apply the relevance of the day's reading to faith communities. Just remember, a faith community may be as large as a regular organized gathering of any religious tradition, or as small as a family, or the relationship between spiritual friends. You don't need to be a member of a church, synagogue, mosque, or temple to be part of a faith community. Answer the questions in the context of your particular faith community.

Then move on to the heading *Psalm Fragment.* Here you will find a brief verse or two from the Hebrew book of Psalms that relate to the day's reading. The Psalms have always been the mainstay of monastic prayer in the Christian tradition and thus a mainstay of Kathleen Norris's life as a Benedictine oblate.

Reflect for a moment on the *Psalm Fragment* and then continue on to the heading *Journal Reflections.* Several suggestions for journaling are given that apply the readings to your own personal experience. It is in journaling that the "day" reaches its climax and the potential for transformative change is greatest. It would be best to buy a separate journal rather than use the *Notes* section of the book. For a journal you can use a spiral-bound or ring-bound notebook or one of the hardcover journal books sold in stationery stores. Below are some suggestions for how to keep a journal. For now, let's go back to the 40-day journey book.

The *Questions to Ponder* and *Journal Reflection* exercises are meant to assist you in reflecting on the daily reading and scripture quotations. Do not feel that you have to answer every question. You may choose which questions or exercises are most helpful to you. Sometimes a perfectly appropriate response to a question is, "I don't know" or "I'm not sure what I think about that." The important thing is to record your own thoughts and questions.

After *Journal Reflections*, you will find two more headings. The first is *Prayers of Hope & Healing*. As a member of a religious community, Kathleen Norris knows well that one of the highest services a Christian can perform is prayer for family and friends, for one's community of faith, for the victims of injustice, and for one's enemies. Under this heading you will find suggestions for prayer that relate to the key points in the day's readings. The last heading (before *Notes*) is *Prayer for Today*, a one or two line prayer to end your "appointment" with Kathleen Norris, and to be prayed from time to time throughout the day.

HINTS ON KEEPING A JOURNAL

A journal is a very helpful tool. Keeping a journal is a form of meditation, a profound way of getting to know yourself—and God—more deeply. Although you could read your 40-day journey book and reflect on it "in your head," writing can help you focus your thoughts, clarify your thinking, and keep a record of your insights, questions, and prayers. Writing is generative: it enables you to have thoughts you would not otherwise have had.

A FEW HINTS FOR JOURNALING

1. Write in your journal with grace. Don't get stuck in trying to do it perfectly. Just write freely. Don't worry about literary style, spelling, or grammar. Your goal is simply to generate thoughts pertinent to your own life and get them down on paper.
2. You may want to begin and end your journaling with prayer. Ask for the guidance and wisdom of the Spirit (and thank God for that guidance and wisdom when you are done).
3. If your journaling takes you in directions that go beyond the journaling questions in your 40-day book, go there. Let the questions encourage, not limit, your writing.
4. Respond honestly. Don't write what you think you're supposed to believe. Write down what you really do believe, in so far as you can identify that. If you don't know, or are not sure, or if you have questions, record those. Questions are often openings to spiritual growth.
5. Carry your 40-day book and journal around with you every day during your journey (only keep them safe from prying eyes). The 40-day journey process is an intense experience that doesn't stop when you close the book. Your mind and heart and spirit will be engaged all day, and it will be helpful to have your book and journal handy to take notes or make new entries as they occur to you.

JOURNEYING WITH OTHERS

You can use your 40-day book with another person, a spiritual friend or partner, or with a small group. It would be best for each person first do his or her own reading, reflection, and writing in solitude. Then when you come together, share the insights you have gained from your time alone. Your discussion will probably focus on the *Questions to Ponder*, however, if the relationship is intimate, you may feel comfortable sharing some of what you have written in your journal. No one, however, should ever be pressured to share anything in their journal if they are not comfortable doing so.

Remember that your goal is to learn from one another, neither to argue, nor to prove that you are right and the other person wrong. Just practice listening and trying to understand why your partner, friend, or colleague thinks as he or she does.

Practicing intercessory prayer together, you will find, will strengthen the spiritual bonds of those who take the journey together. And as you all work to translate insight into action, sharing your experience with each other is a way of encouraging and guiding each other and provides the opportunity to correct each other gently if that becomes necessary.

CONTINUING THE JOURNEY

When the forty days (or forty weeks) are over, a milestone has been reached, but the journey needn't end. One goal of the 40-day series is to introduce you to a particular spiritual guide with the hope that, having whetted your appetite, you will want to keep the journey going. At the end of the book are some suggestions for further reading that will take you deeper on your journey with your mentor.

WHO IS KATHLEEN NORRIS?

In describing her writing process for *Amazing Grace: A Vocabulary of Faith*, Kathleen Norris told a *Homiletics Journal* interviewer that the book needed to start with a chapter on Eschatology (the study of end times). She then went on to say, "Well, I've made a joke now. That's really funny, and some people will get it and others won't." Being a poet, a writer, a preacher, a caregiver, and a careful observer of people and places, Kathleen Norris doesn't write in linear fashion or in chronological order—she looks for the connections between things and places and people.

Both her life and her writing address the challenges many face in trying to answer big questions about who we are, why we are here, and what we are supposed to be doing with our time, our possessions, our talents, and ourselves while we are here. Her writing speaks to and for ordinary people.

Kathleen Norris currently spends her time between Hawaii and South Dakota. When she was a pre-teen, her family moved to Honolulu where her father took a new position as a band director. She now lives in Hawaii again—within walking distance of her mother who is in her late 80s—where they both savor the simple joys of spending time together. Both Kathleen Norris and her mother became widows within the past few years.

When Kathleen's husband, David Dwyer, also a poet, began to decline in health and could no longer make the long commutes from South Dakota to Hawaii, she and David moved to Hawaii from South Dakota. Prior to that, they had made regular trips to Hawaii and spent a portion of each year there, but their permanent home was in Lemmon, South Dakota, where they lived in the home where her mother was raised and where her grandparents lived until they died.

After Norris's grandparents died, she and David moved to South Dakota from their home in New York City, thinking that they would stay in South

Dakota for a few years at the most. In the end, however, they lived there together for over twenty-five years.

After moving to Lemmon, Kathleen Norris ended her twenty-year adult absence from the faith of her grandparents and parents. She began attending the Presbyterian Church where her grandmother had been a member for over sixty years. Although she grew up thinking religion was for children and the elderly—"real" adults had no need for such things—she discovered in Lemmon that she could indeed be both a writer and a person of faith.

It is Kathleen Norris's journey of spiritual self-discovery and re-connection with her family's religious heritage that led to her to write her first nonfiction work: *Dakota: A Spiritual Geography.* The book is a combination journal, travelogue, theology, devotional, and a description of the difficult challenges of trying to survive in the Great Plains. Norris' poetic skills enable us to see much more than the eye alone could ever reveal about the people and the places described in *Dakota.*

Her spiritual journey led her to a Benedictine community in North Dakota. It also led her to the pulpit of the small rural church where her grandmother had worshipped. There she was told, "You're a writer. You can preach." And preach she did when the church was between pastors.

In 1986 she became an oblate, a non-residential member, of the Benedictine community at Assumption Abbey in North Dakota. Her association with the Benedictines continued to deepen when she was accepted into the Institute for Ecumenical and Cultural Research at St. John's Abbey and University in Collegeville, Minnesota, where she spent two nine month terms studying and living within the liturgical prayer life of the monastic community. Her experience and learning is profoundly and beautifully recorded in *The Cloister Walk.* In this beautiful and poetic book, we are treated to a close up view of the daily life of those who live in a monastic community. She weaves together a fascinating portrait of monastic life with insightful connections that apply to those of us who do not and probably never will experience such communal living.

By the time she finished these two books, Norris was ready to write about the challenges of coming back to the church after her twenty-year absence. In *Amazing Grace* she writes in down-to-earth language about her fear of opening the sanctuary door and wondering what would happen to her and her marriage once she entered. The people those in the church too often label "inactives" will find a companion in Kathleen Norris should they decide to attempt re-entry into a faith community.

In *Amazing Grace* she defines and reflects on common church vocabulary that to those outside or on the edges of faith often sounds strange or hopelessly out of touch with the rest of culture. Using her considerable skills as both a poet and a student of the root meaning and origin of words, Norris defines such term as "sin," "grace," "repentance," "dogma," and "faith" in ways that profoundly open us to their meanings and relevance. Through her reflections on such theological terms, we gain a much clearer understanding of the vibrant linkages between faith talk and daily life.

After writing these three faith-focused books, Norris wrote her autobiography, *The Virgin of Bennington*. The title refers to Bennington, Vermont, where she lived while attending the University of Vermont after graduating from high school in Hawaii. As is common for many young people who want to launch out on their own, Norris selected the University of Vermont because it was as far away from home as she could get and still be in the same country, and because it had a writing program.

In *The Virgin of Bennington*, Norris writes about her sheltered life growing up in Virginia, Illinois, and Hawaii. She writes about her life with poet husband David in the artistic community of New York City. She writes about their decision to move into her ancestral home in South Dakota. (Though she never lived in South Dakota during her childhood, she spent many summers there with her grandparents.)

Along the way, Norris has built a solid reputation as an award-winning poet, author, and popular speaker. (*Dakota, The Cloister Walk, Amazing Grace* and *The Virgin of Bennington* were all *New York Times* bestsellers.) She won the 1971 Big Table Younger Poets Award for her first book of poems entitled *Falling Off. Dakota* was named the *New York Times* Book of the Year and selected as one of the best books of the year by the *Library Journal*.

Norris is a welcome speaker at a variety of events from religious leadership conferences to theological seminars to chaplains' groups. Her life, writing, preaching, and lecturing have been compared to the life and works of both Thomas Merton and Hildegard von Bingen. In an age in which we value speed, newness, and rapid change, Norris's willingness to stay still, to listen for God's still small voice, and to cherish the past—both her own personal family history and the 1500-year-old traditions of the Benedictine community—are rare gifts for those who will accept them. As you will discover in what follows, Kathleen Norris shows us how to journey at the speed of life and love.

40-DAY
Journey

WITH KATHLEEN NORRIS

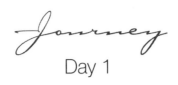

Day 1

THE GREAT COMMANDMENT, TO LOVE God with all your heart and soul, and your neighbor as yourself, seemed more subtle than ever. I began to see the three elements as a kind of trinity, always in motion, and the three loves as interdependent. It would be impossible to love God without loving others; impossible to love others unless one were grounded in a healthy self-respect; and, maybe, impossible to truly love at all in a totally secular way, without participating in the holy.

ᔐ

BIBLICAL WISDOM

Hear, O Israel: The LORD is our God, the LORD alone. You shall love the LORD your God with all your heart, and with all your soul, and with all your might. Deuteronomy 6:4-5

SILENCE FOR MEDITATION

QUESTIONS TO PONDER

- What do you think Kathleen Norris means when she says that it may be "impossible to truly love at all in a totally secular way, without participating in the holy"?
- How can a community of faith actively (and practically) promote love of God, love of the self, and love of the neighbor?
- How should one think about religiously sanctioned violence in the light of the Great Commandment to love?

PSALM FRAGMENT

Steadfast love and faithfulness will meet;
  righteousness and peace will kiss each other. Psalm 85:10

Journal Reflections

- As you begin your 40-day journey with Kathleen Norris, reflect in your journal on your present understanding of what it means for you to love God.
- Reflect on your present understanding of what it means to love yourself.
- Reflect on your present understanding of what it means to love others, and then write about how these three loves are connected for you.

Prayers of Hope & Healing

Thank God for all the people you love and who love you (name them); pray that your love for them and their love for you might deepen and be an expression of your love for God.

Prayer for Today

Loving God, help me to understand and teach me to practice the love that leads to life.

Notes

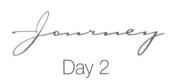

Day 2

WHEN I FIRST STUMBLED UPON the Benedictine abbey where I am now an oblate, I was surprised to find the monks so unconcerned with my weighty doubts and intellectual frustrations over Christianity. What interested them more was my desire to come to their worship, the liturgy of the hours. I was a bit disappointed—I had thought that my doubts were spectacular obstacles to my faith and was confused but intrigued when an old monk blithely stated that doubt is merely the seed of faith, a sign that faith is alive and ready to grow. I am grateful now for his wisdom and grateful to the community for teaching me about the power of liturgy. They seemed to believe that if I just kept coming back to worship, kept coming home, things would eventually fall into place.

BIBLICAL WISDOM

Now the eleven disciples went to Galilee, to the mountain to which Jesus had directed them. When they saw him, they worshiped him; but some doubted.
Matthew 28:16-17

SILENCE FOR MEDITATION

QUESTIONS TO PONDER

- How are people who express doubts about faith, tradition, or practice regarded in your faith community?
- To what extent are people free to express negative thoughts, moods, feelings, or concerns in your family or faith community? How do you think this impacts the family or community?
- In what ways does your community of faith either encourage or discourage people who are exploring what they believe or struggling with their questions of faith?

Psalm Fragment

O God, you are my God, I seek you,
my soul thirsts for you;
my flesh faints for you,
as in a dry and weary land where there is no water.
So I have looked upon you in the sanctuary,
beholding your power and glory. Psalm 63:1-2

Journal Reflections

- Make a list in your journal of any questions or doubts you have about Christian faith and practice. Explore your questions and doubts by writing as much as you can about them. Is there anyone you could talk to about them?
- If doubt is indeed "the seed of faith," is doubt causing any new seeds to sprout in your life of faith? If so, what are they?
- For Kathleen Norris, "the power of liturgy" sustained her growing faith in spite of doubts and confusion. Write about the place of worship in your life of faith.

Prayers of Hope & Healing

Pray for people who have questions about their faith but don't know where (or perhaps how) to ask them.

Prayer for Today

Thank you gracious God that you have faith in me even when I falter and stumble in my faith in you. Help me accept my doubts as part of my spiritual growth.

Notes

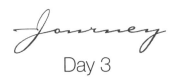

Day 3

IT WAS THE PLAINS THAT first drew me to the monastery, which I suppose is ironic, for who would go seeking a desert within a desert? Both Plains and monastery are places where distractions are at a minimum and you must rely on your own resources, only to find yourself utterly dependent on forces beyond your control; where time seems to stand still, as it does in the liturgy; where your life is defined by waiting.

～

BIBLICAL WISDOM

Then Job answered the LORD:
"I know that you can do all things,
*   and that no purpose of yours can be thwarted.*
'Who is this that hides counsel without knowledge?'
Therefore I have uttered what I did not understand,
*   things too wonderful for me, which I did not know."* Job 42:1-3

SILENCE FOR MEDITATION

QUESTIONS TO PONDER

- What does our culture teach about waiting? Do you agree? Why or why not?
- In your faith community is waiting considered a virtue or an irritation? Explain and give some examples.
- What are some situations in your faith community where "you must rely on your own resources, only to find yourself utterly dependent on forces beyond your control"?

Psalm Fragment

He turns a desert into pools of water,
a parched land into springs of water.
And there he lets the hungry live... Psalm 107:35-36a

Journal Reflections

- Describe a time of waiting for something that was totally out of your control. How did you respond to that time of waiting? Did you learn anything from waiting?
- Is there anything you're waiting for now? If so, what are your thoughts and feelings about this time of waiting?
- What might God be waiting on from you? What will you do about it?

Prayers of Hope & Healing

Pray for those whose well-being and hope for the future depend on the actions of others that they may experience God's presence with them in the time of waiting.

Prayer for Today

God of the past, the present, and the future grant me patience when I must wait, courage when it's time to take action, and the wisdom to know when to wait and when to act.

Notes

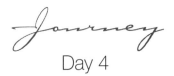
Day 4

BENEDICT'S ADMONISHMENT TO "BEAR WITH the greatest patience the infirmities of others," often acts like fresh air blowing into what could be the ultimate closed system, the smallest small town. Benedict was well aware that, as he put it, "thorns of contention are likely to spring up" in communal living and he recommends as a remedy reciting the Lord's Prayer at both morning and evening office each day. "Thus warned by the pledge they make to one another in the very words of this prayer: *Forgive us as we forgive,*" he writes, the monks may "cleanse themselves of this kind of vice."

~

BIBLICAL WISDOM

Do not judge, so that you may not be judged. For with the judgment you make you will be judged, and the measure you give will be the measure you get. Why do you see the speck in your neighbor's eye, but do not notice the log in your own eye? Matthew 7:1-3

SILENCE FOR MEDITATION

QUESTIONS TO PONDER

- Have there been conflicts within your community that have led people to leave or refuse to work together? What do you think the real issues were?
- How does your faith community or family handle conflict?
- Have you witnessed reconciliation and forgiveness in your family or community? What were the factors that allowed that to happen?

Psalm Fragment

Come and hear, all you who fear God,
*   and I will tell what he has done for me.*
I cried aloud to him,
*   and he was extolled with my tongue.*
If I had cherished iniquity in my heart,
*   the Lord would not have listened.*
But truly God has listened;
*   he has given heed to the words of my prayer.* Psalm 66:16-19

Journal Reflections

- Write about a time when you found yourself bearing "with the greatest patience the infirmities of others." Was it easy or difficult? What did you learn from the experience?
- Write about a time when you experienced the forgiveness of someone else. What was it like for you? Were you changed by the experience?
- Write about a time when you truly forgave someone else? What was that like for you?

Prayers of Hope & Healing

Pray for those who hold grudges that they may be able to embrace the love and forgiveness that only God can provide and seek reconciliation with those they are in conflict with.

Prayer for Today

Gentle God, help me trust you to remove the attitudes and thoughts that prevent me from offering and receiving forgiveness.

Notes

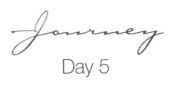

Day 5

WE ARE SEEKING THE TRIBAL, anything with strong communal values and traditions. But all too often we're trying to do it on our own, as individuals. That is the tradition of middle-class America; a belief in individual accomplishment so strong that it favors exploitation over stewardship, mobility over stability.

~

BIBLICAL WISDOM

Just then a lawyer stood up to test Jesus. "Teacher," he said, "what must I do to inherit eternal life?" He said to him, "What is written in the law? What do you read there?" He answered, "You shall love the Lord your God with all your heart, and with all your soul, and with all your strength, and with all your mind; and your neighbor as yourself." And he said to him, "You have given the right answer; do this, and you will live." But wanting to justify himself, he asked Jesus, "And who is my neighbor?" Luke 10:25-29

SILENCE FOR MEDITATION

QUESTIONS TO PONDER

- How would you rate your community's awareness of, concern for, and action on behalf of those who are struggling? Could more be done?
- Our culture often promotes a "dog-eat-dog," "winner takes all," "losers get nothing" approach to life. Does your community of faith sanction or challenge this attitude? Explain.
- How could both your faith community and the larger community in which you live promote stewardship over exploitation and stability over mobility?

PSALM FRAGMENT

How very good and pleasant it is
when kindred live together in unity!...
For there the LORD ordained his blessing,
life forevermore. Psalm 133:1,3b

JOURNAL REFLECTIONS

- Do you know your neighbors? Why or why not? How do you feel about this?
- Where do you experience the strongest sense of fitting in and belonging? Why?
- What might be some ways God is nudging you to show concern for your neighbors?

PRAYERS OF HOPE & HEALING

Pray for those who live alone, that they may find places to experience community. Pray for those who seek only their own advantage that they may find joy in seeking the advantage of others.

PRAYER FOR TODAY

Lord God, you call us together into the one body of Jesus Christ. Use me to welcome the stranger and newcomers in my community.

NOTES

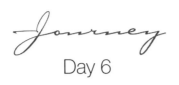

Day 6

IN ANY TRADITIONAL SOCIETY, STORIES are where the life is, where those in the present maintain continuity with those in the past. In the monastic tradition, from the fourth-century desert on, it is the stories that pass from monk to monk, long before they're written down, that have helped preserve the values, and the good humor, that lives on in the monastic charism.

~

BIBLICAL WISDOM

And as for the dead being raised, have you not read in the book of Moses, in the story about the bush, how God said to him, 'I am the God of Abraham, the God of Isaac, and the God of Jacob'? He is God not of the dead, but of the living... Mark 12:26-27

SILENCE FOR MEDITATION

QUESTIONS TO PONDER

- What are some of the stories that get told over and over again in your faith community? What does the telling of these stories accomplish?
- Who are the main storytellers in your community? Why were they given this role?
- Are there some stories in your community that are carefully guarded from newcomers? If so, why?

PSALM FRAGMENT

I will give thanks to the LORD with my whole heart;
    I will tell of all your wonderful deeds.
I will be glad and exult in you;
    I will sing praise to your name, O Most High. Psalm 9:1-2

Journal Reflections

- Try writing a brief faith history of your family. How have the faith stories of your family helped to shape who you are?
- What are your favorite family stories? How do these stories "preserve the values, and the good humor," and the uniqueness of your family?
- What biblical stories best connect with your personal stories? Why do these stories speak to your experience?

Prayers of Hope & Healing

Pray for individuals, families, and communities with shameful stories that destroy their spirit and joy that they may find in the story of Jesus' life, death, and resurrection the courage to confess their secrets and be healed of their shame.

Prayer for Today

God of history, thank you for the many generations in my family and for all the stories I have heard about these men and women who are an important part of my own story.

Notes

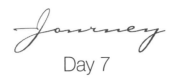

Day 7

HER (KATHLEEN NORRIS'S GRANDMOTHER TOTTEN) faith was alive for anyone to see; her life demonstrates that conversion is no more spectacular than learning to love the people we live with and work among. It does not mean seeking out the most exotic spiritual experience, or the ideal religion, the holiest teachers who will give us the greatest return on our investment. Conversion is seeing ourselves, and the ordinary people in our families, our classrooms, and on the job, in a new light. Can it be that these very people—even the difficult, unbearable ones—are the ones God has given us, so that together we might find salvation?

~

BIBLICAL WISDOM

Therefore, my beloved, just as you have always obeyed me, not only in my presence, but much more now in my absence, work out your own salvation with fear and trembling; for it is God who is at work in you, enabling you both to will and to work for his good pleasure. Philippians 2:12-13

SILENCE FOR MEDITATION

QUESTIONS TO PONDER

- Read Romans 13:8-10. Does your community of faith promote the way of life Paul—and Kathleen Norris's grandmother—is advocating? If yes, in what ways? If not, what might be done?
- Every community has some every day heroes—men and women whose lives have a profound and positive impact on their community—one they are often not even aware of. Who are these people in your community? What character traits do they have that explains their impact?
- In what ways might the troublesome, difficult people in your community be revealing God's presence among you?

Psalm Fragment

How precious is your steadfast love, O God!
All people may take refuge in the shadow of your wings.
They feast on the abundance of your house,
and you give them drink from the river of your delights.
For with you is the fountain of life;
in your light we see light. Psalm 36:7-9

Journal Reflections

- Make a list of the people who have influenced you most in your faith journey. After each name write a paragraph explaining their influence on you.
- In what ways are you "learning to love the people [you] live with and work among"?
- Have any of the difficult people in your life helped you come to a deeper appreciation of God's presence in your life? If so, how did they help and what did you learn/experience?

Prayers of Hope & Healing

Pray for the common, ordinary saints who inspire you by their faithful lives and quiet witness to their faith in God. Pray for "the difficult, unbearable ones" that together you may find salvation.

Prayer for Today

God of my ancestors, thank you for the faith that has been passed down to me by those before me. Make me mindful of what witness I am giving those who will follow me.

Notes

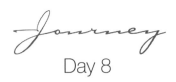

Day 8

THE HEBREW WORD FOR "SALVATION" means literally "to make wide," or "to make sufficient," and our friend had recognized that the road he has taken was not wise enough to sustain his life; it was sufficient only as a way leading to death. . . The Hebrew words usually come from a military context, and refer to victory over evil or rescue from danger in this life. And in the gospels it is often physical healing that people seek from Jesus, relief from blindness, paralysis, leprosy. When he says to them that their faith has saved them, it is the Greek word for "made you well" that is employed. It seems right to me that in so many instances in both the Hebrew Scriptures and the gospels salvation is described in physical terms, in terms of the here and now, because I believe that this is how most of us first experience it.

BIBLICAL WISDOM

As Jesus went on from there, two blind men followed him, crying loudly, "Have mercy on us, Son of David!" When he entered the house, the blind men came to him; and Jesus said to them, "Do you believe that I am able to do this?" They said to him, "Yes, Lord." Then he touched their eyes and said, "According to your faith let it be done to you." And their eyes were opened. Matthew 9:27-30a.

SILENCE FOR MEDITATION

QUESTIONS TO PONDER

- What does your community of faith teach about the connection between salvation and physical healing or well-being?
- What role do you think faith plays in healing? How do you explain people who pray for healing, but remain ill or die anyway?
- Does your community of faith teach salvation primarily in terms of eternal life or equally "in terms of the here and now"? What value might there be in stressing the "here and now-ness" of salvation?

PSALM FRAGMENT

Blessed be the LORD,
  who daily bears us up;
  God is our salvation.
Our God is a God of salvation,
  and to GOD, the LORD, belongs escape from death. Psalm 68:19-20

JOURNAL REFLECTIONS

- Reflect on the biblical words for salvation that Kathleen Norris explains, and then write about your own present understanding of salvation. In what ways, if any, do you experience God's salvation in the "here and now"?
- Write about a time when you where seriously ill or in serious trouble. How did you experience God in those circumstances?
- Reflect on your life journey. Can you see any ways in which God is working "to make wide" or "to make sufficient" the path you are taking?

PRAYERS OF HOPE & HEALING

Pray for all who suffer illness in mind, body, or spirit that they may experience the salvation of God. Pray for those who seem lost on life's journey that they may find God preparing a wide and sufficient path for them.

PRAYER FOR TODAY

God, our great physician, help me take care of the body, mind, and spirit that you have given me and trust you with the results of my efforts. May I walk today the sufficient path you prepare before me.

NOTES

Day 9

PERFECTIONISM IS ONE OF THE scariest words I know. It is a marked characteristic of contemporary American culture, a serious psychological affliction that makes people too timid to take necessary risks and causes them to suffer when, although they've done the best they can, their efforts fall short of some imaginary, and usually unattainable, standard. . . The word that has been translated as "perfect" does not mean to set forth an impossible goal, or the perfectionism that would have me strive for it at any cost. It is taken from a Latin word meaning complete, entire, full-grown. To those who originally heard it, the word would convey "mature" rather than what we mean today by "perfect."

BIBLICAL WISDOM

For if you love those who love you, what reward do you have? Do not even the tax collectors do the same? And if you greet only your brothers and sisters, what more are you doing than others? Do not even the Gentiles do the same? Be perfect, therefore, as your heavenly Father is perfect. Matthew 5:46-48

SILENCE FOR MEDITATION

QUESTIONS TO PONDER

- How does our culture (and religion) understand perfection? How do you understand perfection?
- Do you think the expectations of people in your community of faith are too tough, too lenient, or just about right? Explain.
- How can a faith community balance accountability and quality with grace?

PSALM FRAGMENT

This God—his way is perfect;
   the promise of the LORD proves true;
   he is a shield for all who take refuge in him. Psalm 18:30

JOURNAL REFLECTIONS

- Do you struggle with fears about being found imperfect and therefore not acceptable to others or to God? If so, how do you handle those fears? If not, to what do you attribute your self-acceptance?
- In what ways do you consider yourself "mature"? In what areas of your life do you still need to grow toward greater maturity?
- Describe yourself as though you were another person describing you to someone who doesn't know you. When you're done, look back to see how gracious or how hard you were on yourself.

PRAYERS OF HOPE & HEALING

Pray for those who struggle with perfectionism that they may accept their worth as precious children of God.

PRAYER FOR TODAY

Gracious God, guide my efforts to continue to mature and to trust you to accept me fully when I fail.

NOTES

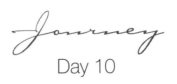
Day 10

I WAS DRAWN TO THE strong old women in the congregation. Their well-worn Bibles said to me, "There is more here than you know." And made me take more seriously the religion that had caused my grandmother Totten's Bible to be so well used that its spine broke. I also began, slowly, to make sense of our gathering together on Sunday morning, recognizing, however dimly, that church is to be participated in and not consumed. The point is not what one gets out of it, but the worship of God; the service takes place both because of and despite the needs, strengths, and frailties of the people present.

⌐

BIBLICAL WISDOM

They devoted themselves to the apostles' teaching and fellowship, to the breaking of bread and the prayers. Awe came upon everyone, because many wonders and signs were being done by the apostles. All who believed were together and had all things in common; they would sell their possessions and goods and distribute the proceeds to all, as any had need. Acts 2:42-45

SILENCE FOR MEDITATION

QUESTIONS TO PONDER

- How can our communities of faith avoid being co-opted by the values of our consumerist society in the way they do worship?
- Kathleen Norris says that "the point (of going to church) is not what one gets out of it, but the worship of God." Do you agree? Why or why not?
- What do you think Kathleen Norris means when she writes: "The service takes place both because of and despite the needs, strengths, and frailties of the people present"?

PSALM FRAGMENT

I was glad when they said to me, "Let us go to the house of the Lord!"
Psalm 122:1

JOURNAL REFLECTIONS

- Write about your experience of worship—the negative as well as the positive. Is there anything you might do to enhance your worship experience?
- Where (and/or with whom) do you most experience the presence of God? Write about the places and relationships where you are most aware of God's presence.
- Kathleen Norris wrote that she "was drawn to the strong old women in the congregation. Their well-worn Bibles said to me, 'There is more here than you know.'" Write about your feelings about the Bible and how you do—or don't—use it to sustain and guide your life. Is there more you might do?

PRAYERS OF HOPE & HEALING

Pray for all who serve God by serving their congregations that they may find joy and meaning in the smallest acts of love. Pray for all who gather in worship that they would encounter the living God in the liturgy, the hymns, the sermon, and the sacraments.

PRAYER FOR TODAY

Dear God, grant me the discipline to read your word and the willingness to hear what you would teach me through it.

NOTES

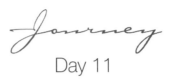

Day 11

THE GREEK ROOT FROM WHICH "dogma" comes means "what seems good, fitting, becoming." Thus, the word "beauty" might be a more fitting synonym for dogma than what has become its synonym in contemporary English: "doctrine," or a teaching. . . . [W]hen dogma is in its proper place, as beauty, it appeals to my poetic sensibility, rather than to my more linear intelligence. I have a hard time, in fact, separating "dogma" out from the sheer joy of worship. At its best, the sights and sounds of worship, its stories, poems, hymns, and liturgical actions, are beautiful in the sense of "good, fitting, becoming."

⁓

BIBLICAL WISDOM

Again he entered the synagogue, and a man was there who had a withered hand. They watched him to see whether he would cure him on the Sabbath, so that they might accuse him. And he said to the man who had the withered hand, "Come forward." Then he said to them, "Is it lawful to do good or to do harm on the Sabbath, to save life or to kill?" But they were silent. He looked around at them with anger; he was grieved at their hardness of heart and said to the man, "Stretch out your hand." He stretched it out, and his hand was restored. Mark 3: 2-5

SILENCE FOR MEDITATION

QUESTIONS TO PONDER

- Following Kathleen Norris's understanding, does your community of faith see "dogma" as doctrine or as beauty (or perhaps as both)? Which understanding appeals most to you? Why?
- In your community of faith, do you experience "the sights and sounds of worship, its stories, poems, hymns, and liturgical actions, [as] beautiful in the sense of 'good, fitting, becoming'"? Why or why not?
- What differences might there be between our culture's understanding of beauty and a more religious understanding of beauty?

PSALM PORTION

One thing I asked of the LORD,
that will I seek after:
to live in the house of the LORD
all the days of my life,
to behold the beauty of the LORD,
and to inquire in his temple. Psalm 27:4

JOURNAL REFLECTIONS

- Write about those things/experiences in your life of faith that you find beautiful.
- Is worship both beautiful and a learning experience for you? Why or why not?
- In what ways, if any, do the beauty and teaching of worship carry over into your everyday life?

PRAYERS OF HOPE & HEALING

Pray for those who plan and lead worship that they may both be drawn into its beauty and enable others to experience that beauty.

PRAYER FOR TODAY

God of beauty, may my life reflect your beauty and be a continuing act of worship.

NOTES

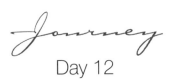
Day 12

VERY FEW (CHILDREN) WROTE WITH any originality about making noise. Most of their images were clichés such as "we sound like a herd of elephants." But silence was another matter: here their images often had a depth and maturity that was unlike anything else they wrote. One boy came up with an image of strength as being "as low and silent as a tree," another wrote that "silence is me sleeping waiting to wake up. Silence is a tree spreading its branches to the sun." In a parochial school, one third grader's poem turned into a prayer: "Silence is spiders spinning their webs; it's like a silkworm making its silk. Lord, help me to know when to be silent." And in a tiny town in western North Dakota a little girl offered a gem of spiritual wisdom that I find myself returning to when my life becomes too noisy and distractions overwhelm me: "Silence reminds me to take my soul with me wherever I go."

BIBLICAL WISDOM

He said, "Go out and stand on the mountain before the LORD, for the LORD is about to pass by." Now there was a great wind, so strong that it was splitting mountains and breaking rocks in pieces before the LORD, but the LORD was not in the wind; and after the wind an earthquake, but the LORD was not in the earthquake; and after the earthquake a fire, but the LORD was not in the fire; and after the fire a sound of sheer silence. 1 Kings 19:11-12

SILENCE FOR MEDITATION

QUESTIONS TO PONDER

- In what ways does our culture discourage silence? Why? How might people begin to overcome the discomfort with—if not fear of—silence, which seems so pervasive in our society?

- Does your community of faith provide and encourage the use of quiet places away from noise and daily distractions? If yes, how? If not, what might be done?
- In your faith community, how is silence used in worship? Could it be used more effectively? If so, how?

PSALM FRAGMENT

"Be still, and know that I am God;
I will be exalted among the nations,
I will be exalted in the earth!" Psalm 46:10

JOURNAL REFLECTIONS

- Write about whether or not you are comfortable with silence.
- Remember a time of silence you experienced in the past. What thoughts, feelings, and memories does this stir for you?
- Does God seem closer to you or further away in times of silence? Why? How might you build more times of solitude and silence into your life?

PRAYERS OF HOPE & HEALING

Pray for those whose lives are filled with noise and distractions that they may discover the silence within which God is known in love.

PRAYER FOR TODAY

Gracious God, help me learn to accept times of silence as opportunities to be more aware of your companionship.

NOTES

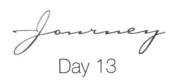

Day 13

MONKS ARE NOT USED TO being compared to camels in heat, but they took it pretty well. I noticed eyebrows going up around the choir, and then a kind of quiet assent: *well, there are days.* Monks know very well how easy it is to lose track of one's purpose in life, how hard to maintain the discipline that keeps (in St. Benedict's words) "our minds in harmony with our voices" in prayer, the ease with which aimless desire can disturb our hearts. "Stop wearing out your shoes" (Jeremiah 2:25). *Stop wearing out your shoes.* Good advice for us in America, in a society grown alarmingly mobile, where retreats and spirituality workshops have become such a hot consumer item one wonders if seeking the holy has become an end in itself.

BIBLICAL WISDOM

How can you say, "I am not defiled, I have not gone after the Baals"? Look at your way in the valley; know what you have done—a restive young camel interlacing her tracks, a wild ass at home in the wilderness, in her heat sniffing the wind! Who can restrain her lust? None who seek her need weary themselves; in her month they will find her. Keep your feet from going unshod and your throat from thirst. But you said, "It is hopeless, for I have loved strangers (false gods), and after them I will go." Jeremiah 2:23-25

SILENCE FOR MEDITATION

QUESTIONS TO PONDER

- The problem of people chasing after false gods didn't end with the ancient people. What are the false gods and aimless desires you see people chasing after today?
- In what ways, if any, does your community of faith help people identify and challenge the false gods and aimless desires that distract us from following God?

- In our culture, what would it look like if we followed Jeremiah's advice to "stop wearing out your shoes" or "do not run until your feet are bare"?

PSALM FRAGMENT

Many times he delivered them,
*   but they were rebellious in their purposes,*
*   and were brought low through their iniquity.*
Nevertheless he regarded their distress
*   when he heard their cry.* Psalm 106:43-44

JOURNAL REFLECTIONS

- Kathleen Norris speaks of "the ease with which aimless desire can disturb our hearts." Is your heart disturbed? If so, what by? What might you do about it? If not, what is it that gives your heart rest and peace?
- Our multi-tasking culture seems to fast-track everything. Are there days when you feel like you're running just to stay even and your shoes are wearing out? Do you want to slow down? If so, how can you slow down?
- Describe your vision of a healthy spiritual life. If you have not realized this vision, what might you do to move in the direction of the spiritual life you envision?

PRAYERS OF HOPE & HEALING

Pray for all who are harried and distracted with chasing after "false gods" and "aimless desires" that they may find the grace to slow down and be open to the presence of God in everyday things and relationships.

PRAYER FOR TODAY

Dear God, I love to go faster than is good for me or for my relationship with you. Help me slow down so I don't miss what you want to give me.

NOTES

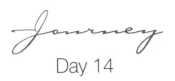

Day 14

VERY SMALL CHILDREN ARE OFTEN conscious of God, for example, in ways that adults seldom are. They sing to God, they talk to God, they recognize divine presence in the world around them: they can see the Virgin Mary dancing among the clouds, they know that God made a deep ravine by their house "because he was angry when people would not love him," they believe that an overnight snowfall is "just like Jesus glowing on the mountaintop."

⌒

BIBLICAL WISDOM

People were bringing little children to him in order that he might touch them; and the disciples spoke sternly to them. But when Jesus saw this, he was indignant and said to them, "Let the little children come to me; do not stop them; for it is to such as these that the kingdom of God belongs. Truly I tell you, whoever does not receive the kingdom of God as a little child will never enter it." And he took them up in his arms, laid his hands on them, and blessed them. Mark 10:13-16

SILENCE FOR MEDITATION

QUESTIONS TO PONDER

- How does your faith community respond to families with small children? What's your nursery like? How do people react when a child makes noise during worship?
- What role do children and youth play in your worship services? Could that role be expanded? If so, how? If not, why not?
- What opportunities do children have to talk about their faith in your community?

PSALM FRAGMENT

Sing praises to God, sing praises;
*   sing praises to our King, sing praises.*
For God is the king of all the earth;
*   sing praises with a psalm.* Psalm 47:6-7

JOURNAL REFLECTIONS

- Spend some time remembering and meditating upon your early childhood. What kind of spiritual experiences did you have? Did you feel like God was close to you? How did you experience God?
- Write God a "Dear God, This is (fill in your own name)" letter. Thank God for something or someone in your life using (as best you can) the language of a small child.
- Write a blessing for a child in your life. If there are no children in your life, write a blessing for the children of your faith community.

PRAYERS OF HOPE & HEALING

Pray for the children among us that we may keep them safe, respect their spiritual experience, and learn from their direct ways of relating to and talking to God.

PRAYER FOR TODAY

Lord God, how quick I am to forget that you love me as a loving parent. Let me trust you, talk to you, and sing to you the way a child is with a caring parent.

NOTES

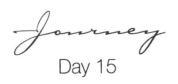
Day 15

PRAYER WAS IMPOSSIBLE FOR ME for years. For a time I was so alienated from my religious heritage that I had the vainglorious notion that somehow, if I prayed, I would cause more harm than good. But when a priest I knew asked me to pray for him—he'd been diagnosed with a serious illness—my "yes" was immediate, sincere, and complete. I wasn't sure that I could pray well and was shocked that the priest would trust me to do so. But I recognized that this was my pride speaking, the old perfectionism that has dogged me since I was a child. Well, or badly, that was beside the point. Of course I could pray, and I did.

ᕀ

BIBLICAL WISDOM

Two men went up to the temple to pray, one a Pharisee and the other a tax collector. The Pharisee, standing by himself, was praying thus, 'God, I thank you that I am not like other people: thieves, rogues, adulterers, or even like this tax collector. I fast twice a week; I give a tenth of all my income.' But the tax collector, standing far off, would not even look up to heaven, but was beating his breast and saying, 'God, be merciful to me, a sinner!' I tell you, this man went down to his home justified rather than the other; for all who exalt themselves will be humbled, but all who humble themselves will be exalted. Luke 18:10-14

SILENCE FOR MEDITATION

QUESTIONS TO PONDER

- What is the climate for prayer in your faith community? Open or closed? Formal or informal? Reserved for the professionals or inclusive of all?
- In what ways does your community of faith encourage and teach the practice of prayer? Could more be done? If so, what?
- Do the people in your faith community seem generally comfortable or uncomfortable with prayer? Explain. If uncomfortable, what might be done to raise the comfort level?

PSALM FRAGMENT

Answer me when I call, O God of my right!
  You gave me room when I was in distress.
  Be gracious to me, and hear my prayer. Psalm 4:1

JOURNAL REFLECTIONS

- Write about the place of prayer in your life. Is it important and meaningful to you?
- Does praying come easily for you or not so easily? How often do you pray? Where do you pray? What do you usually pray about?
- Are there kinds of prayer you would like to know more about? Is there someone who could help you learn more about the practice of prayer? How could you work more time for prayer into your daily life?

PRAYERS OF HOPE & HEALING

Pray for those who are called upon to pray for others as part of their role in the church or society that their witness might inspire others to pray as well.

PRAYER FOR TODAY

Dear God, help me remember that prayer is a two-way conversation and to take time to listen as well as to speak.

NOTES

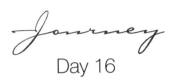

Day 16

I BECAME AWARE OF THREE paradoxes in the psalms: (1) that in them pain is indeed "missed—in Praise," but in a way that takes pain fully into account; (2) that though of all the books of the Bible the psalms speak most directly to the individual, they cannot be removed from a communal context; (3) and that the psalms are holistic in insisting that the mundane and the holy are inextricably linked. The Benedictine method of reading psalms, with long silences between them rather than commentary or explanation, takes full advantage of these paradoxes, offering almost alarming room for interpretation and response.

BIBLICAL WISDOM

All scripture is inspired by God and is useful for teaching, for reproof, for correction, and for training in righteousness, so that everyone who belongs to God may be proficient, equipped for every good work. 2 Timothy 3:16-17

SILENCE FOR MEDITATION

QUESTIONS TO PONDER

- In a monastic community, reciting and meditating on the psalms are central in the worship and prayer life of the community. How are the psalms read or used in your faith community?
- Do you agree with Kathleen Norris's statement that the psalms are "holistic in insisting that the mundane and the holy are inextricably linked"? Why or why not?
- How might the psalms help us, both individually and as a community of faith, to address all of the violence and suffering in our world?

PSALM FRAGMENT

Search me, O God, and know my heart;
test me and know my thoughts.
See if there is any wicked way in me,
and lead me in the way everlasting. Psalm 139:23-24

JOURNAL REFLECTIONS

- Reflect on your life. Have you ever had an experience where your very real pain or suffering was "missed—in Praise"? If so, write about the experience. If not, try to imagine how such an experience might be possible.
- Try writing a letter to someone you care about using as many images from the psalms as you can. Do these images help to link the "mundane and the holy" for you?
- Kathleen Norris refers to the "Benedictine method of reading psalms, with long silences between them (for interpretation and response) rather than commentary or explanation." If you have had such an experience, what was it like for you? If you haven't, is there a small group of people you could try it with?

PRAYERS OF HOPE & HEALING

Pray for musicians who set the psalms to music for us to sing that these ancient poems might be a source of strength, comfort, and wisdom for them.

PRAYER FOR TODAY

Thank you God for inspiring the authors of the psalms that speak to me today; let me be as open and honest with you as they were.

NOTES

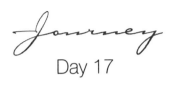
Day 17

THE PSALMS REVEAL OUR MOST difficult conflicts, and our deep desire, in Jungian terms, to run from the shadow. In them, the shadow speaks to us directly, in words that are painful to hear. In recent years, some Benedictine houses, particularly women's communities, have begun censoring the harshest of the psalms, often called the "cursing psalms," from their public worship. But one sister, a liturgist, said after visiting such a community, "I began to get antsy, feeling, *something is not right*. The human experience is of violence, and the psalms reflect our experience of the world."

BIBLICAL WISDOM

So then, putting away falsehood, let all of us speak the truth to our neighbors, for we are members of one another. Be angry but do not sin; do not let the sun go down on your anger... Ephesians 4:25-26

SILENCE FOR MEDITATION

QUESTIONS TO PONDER

- The psalms contain a lot of angry words; so does modern rap music. What differences do you note between the ways the psalms deal with violence and how it is handled in modern music?
- Violence, as Kathleen Norris notes, is part and parcel of human experience. How do you think religion should respond to the reality of human violence?
- Do you agree with Kathleen Norris's thinking that we shouldn't censor the psalms used in corporate worship? Why or why not?

Psalm Fragment

Have mercy on me, O God,
   according to your steadfast love;
   according to your abundant mercy
   blot out my transgressions. Psalm 51:1

Journal Reflections

- Think of a time when you were really furious with someone one or about some situation. Write a psalm about it—that is, write honestly and openly to God about the feelings and desires that the situation evoked in you.
- Kathleen Norris speaks of the "shadow," the darkness within each of us, the seemingly negative side of ourselves that we would like to run away from. Try to describe your "shadow." Are you in touch with your "shadow"? Can you express your shadow side openly to God? Can you *own* your shadow and still claim and affirm your goodness and trust in God as the psalmists did?
- Write a short psalm to God expressing your current "experience of the world."

Prayers of Hope & Healing

Pray for professionals who work with angry, hostile people in their line of work that they may be safe and find ways to defuse the anger and transform it into hope.

Prayer for Today

God of all goodness and compassion, help me to bring my darkness into your light and live in such a way that I cause no harm to others.

Notes

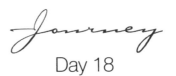

Day 18

THE LITURGY THAT BENEDICTINES HAVE been experimenting with for fifteen-hundred-plus years taught me the value of tradition; I came to see that the psalms are holy in part because they are so well-used. If so many generations had found solace here, might I also? The holiness of the psalms came to seem like that of a stone that has been held in the palm by countless ancestors, illustrating what the poet Galway Kinnell has termed the "merely personal," or individual, and the "truly personal," which is individual experience reflected back into the community and tradition. That great scholar of mysticism, Evelyn Underhill, makes the same distinctions when speaking of prayer, admitting that "devotion by itself has little value. . .and may even be a form of self-indulgence," unless it is accompanied by a transformation of the personal. "The spiritual life of individuals," she writes, "has to be extended both vertically to God and horizontally to other souls; and the more it grows in both directions, the less merely individual and therefore the more truly personal it will be."

BIBLICAL WISDOM

He has told you, O mortal, what is good; and what does the LORD require of you but to do justice, and to love kindness, and to walk humbly with your God?
Micah 6:8

SILENCE FOR MEDITATION

QUESTIONS TO PONDER

- What is the primary emphasis in your faith community—on the vertical relationship with God or the horizontal relationship with others? Or does your faith community maintain a balance between the two? Explain. Where does your emphasis lie?

- What does our culture teach, both positively and negatively, about the "value of tradition"?
- In what ways does your community of faith show that it values tradition? Is your community "tradition bound" or is it free to depart from tradition when and where it seems necessary for faithful worship and service?

PSALM FRAGMENT

Then I said, "Here I am;
in the scroll of the book it is written of me.
I delight to do your will, O my God;
your law is within my heart." Psalm 40: 7-8

JOURNAL REFLECTIONS

- Kathleen Norris writes "the holiness of the psalms came to seem like that of a stone that has been held in the palm by countless ancestors…" Meditate on that image. What feelings does it evoke in you?
- Make a list of the things in your life that are "holy in part because they are so well used."
- Write about the ways your spiritual practice seems to be "accompanied by a transformation of the personal."

PRAYERS OF HOPE & HEALING

Pray for spiritual directors who seek to help people grow in both their devotion to God and their service to others that they may themselves continue to grow in faith and faithfulness.

PRAYER FOR TODAY

Gracious God, may my love for you work itself out in love for others.

NOTES

Journey

Day 19

I HAVE FOUND THAT WHEN I have asked children to write their own psalms, their poems often have an emotional directness that is similar to that of the biblical Psalter. They know what it is like to be small in a world designed for big people, to feel lost and abandoned. Children are frequently astonished to discover that the psalmists so freely express the more unacceptable emotions, sadness and even anger, even anger at God, and that all of this is in the Bible that they hear read in church on Sunday morning

~

BIBLICAL WISDOM

You will be in the right, O LORD,
*   when I lay charges against you;*
*   but let me put my case to you.*
Why does the way of the guilty prosper?
Why do all who are treacherous thrive?
You plant them, and they take root;
*   they grow and bring forth fruit;*
*   you are near in their mouths*
*   yet far from their hearts.* Jeremiah 12:1-2

SILENCE FOR MEDITATION

QUESTIONS TO PONDER

- What is it about children that gives them more "emotional directness" than many adults? How might adults learn to be more emotionally honest with God?
- In your faith community, is emotional honesty with God (even about the "more unacceptable emotions") encouraged or discouraged? In what ways?
- In what ways might oppressed minority Christians find the psalmists' freedom to be emotionally honest a liberating experience?

PSALM FRAGMENT

My God, my God, why have you forsaken me?
Why are you so far from helping me,
  from the words of my groaning?
O my God, I cry by day, but you do not answer,
  and by night, but find no rest. Psalm 22:1-2

JOURNAL REFLECTIONS

- Write about your personal comfort level with expressing the "more unacceptable emotions,…even anger at God," to God.
- Meditate in writing on whether *complete* emotional honesty with God draws you closer to God or distances you from God?
- Think of a time when you wanted to protest to God, "That's not fair!" Write a psalm to God about that situation and reflect on how it makes you feel.

PRAYERS OF HOPE & HEALING

Pray for those who feel lost and abandoned, who struggle with sadness and anger, who feel distanced from God that they might have the courage to express their feelings in the confidence that God is listening in love.

PRAYER FOR TODAY

God of justice and mercy, let me be as concerned about what is fair to my neighbor as I am concerned about what is fair for myself.

NOTES

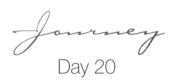

Day 20

THE IDEA OF JUDGMENT, OF being called to account for the way we have lived in the world, is solemn, and terrifying. But as I began to read and meditate on the gospel story [Matthew 13], I could appreciate the way that folk wisdom and ancient agricultural know-how were being used to convey a truth of human psychology. It is consoling to find that nowhere in the text was there the slightest justification for our being judgmental of others. In fact, the parable was a powerful injunction against just that. What I found in the story was a sense that God, knowing us better than we know ourselves, also recognizes that we are incapable of separating the wheat from the weeds in our lives.

BIBLICAL WISDOM

He put before them another parable: "The kingdom of heaven may be compared to someone who sowed good seed in his field; but while everybody was asleep, an enemy came and sowed weeds among the wheat, and then went away. So when the plants came up and bore grain, then the weeds appeared as well... The slaves said to him, 'Then do you want us to go and gather them?' But he replied, 'No; for in gathering the weeds you would uproot the wheat along with them. Let both of them grow together until the harvest; and at harvest time I will tell the reapers, Collect the weeds first and bind them in bundles to be burned, but gather the wheat into my barn.'" Matthew 13:24-29

SILENCE FOR MEDITATION

QUESTIONS TO PONDER

- In light of Kathleen Norris's interpretation of the Matthew text, how should we deal with inappropriate behavior in ourselves and in others?
- In what ways does the theme of judgment play itself out in your community of faith?
- What does our culture teach about the idea of judgment? How should religious communities respond to culture on this point?

PSALM FRAGMENT

May those who sow in tears
reap with shouts of joy.
Those who go out weeping,
bearing the seed for sowing,
shall come home with shouts of joy,
carrying their sheaves. Psalm 126: 5-6

JOURNAL REFLECTIONS

- Meditate in writing about any weeds in your life that are growing along with the good seeds you're trying to nurture.
- Kathleen Norris suggests, "we are incapable of separating the wheat from the weeds in our lives." Write about whether or not you are able to accept this truth and so are able to be gentle with yourself and others.
- Can you think of a time when you were in the wrong and instead of judgment and criticism you encountered grace and acceptance? If so, what lessons does your story contain?

PRAYERS OF HOPE & HEALING

Pray for those who judge themselves and others harshly that they may be comforted and guided by the merciful, forgiving, and transforming grace and acceptance of God.

PRAYER FOR TODAY

God of justice and mercy, help me not judge others and be willing to hear what others tell me about changes that I need to make in my own life.

NOTES

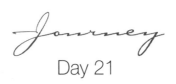

Day 21

THE LITERATURE OF APOCALYPSE [ABOUT the end times and judgment] is scary stuff, the kind of thing that can give religion a bad name, because people so often use it as a means of controlling others, instilling dread by invoking a boogeyman God. Thinking about the people who would be in church that morning, I knew that many of them would very likely be survivors of such painful childhood images of God and would find the readings hard to take. So I decided to talk about what apocalyptic literature is and is not. It is not a detailed prediction of the future, or an invitation to withdraw from the concerns of this world. It is a wake-up call, one that uses intensely poetic language and imagery to sharpen our awareness of God's presence in and promise for the world. The word "apocalypse" comes from the Greek for "uncovering" or "revealing," which makes it a word about possibilities.

⁓

BIBLICAL WISDOM

And I heard a loud voice from the throne saying, "See, the home of God is among mortals. He will dwell with them; they will be his peoples, and God himself will be with them; he will wipe every tear from their eyes. Death will be no more; mourning and crying and pain will be no more, for the first things have passed away." Revelation 21:3-4

SILENCE FOR MEDITATION

QUESTIONS TO PONDER

- Why do you think so many people are concerned with (or worried about) the *end times* in our time? Are such fears warranted?
- Does your faith community proclaim an apocalyptic message? If so, does it generate hope or fear? If not, how is the future talked about in your community?

- In what ways might Kathleen Norris's statement that apocalyptic literature is not a detailed prediction of the future…[but rather] "is a wake-up call… to sharpen our awareness of God's presence in and promise for the world" be a source of strength and confidence for a faith community?

PSALM FRAGMENT

How weighty to me are your thoughts, O God!
  How vast is the sum of them!
I try to count them—they are more than the sand;
  I come to the end—I am still with you. Psalm 139:17-18

JOURNAL REFLECTIONS

- Has anyone ever used the threat of God's final judgment to frighten and control you? If so, write about the experience. How did (do) you respond? If not, what do you think about the use of "fear tactics" in religious proclamation or teaching?
- Have you ever worried about the end of the world and the final judgment of God? If so, write about the feeling. If not, how do you think and feel about such things?
- Are you an apocalyptic thinker? If so, what aspects of our society's political, economic, and social life do you think need "uncovering" or "revealing" in order to disclose greater possibilities for people?

PRAYERS OF HOPE & HEALING

Pray for those who have been threatened, frightened, or intimidated by religious proclamation and teaching that they might know and experience that the perfect love of God casts out all fear.

PRAYER FOR TODAY

God of yesterday, today, and tomorrow, help me to live each moment in the awareness of your loving presence that I may trust in your mercy and not fear death.

NOTES

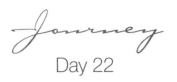

Day 22

GRADUALLY MY PERSPECTIVE ON TIME had changed. In our culture, time can seem like an enemy: it chews us up and spits us out with appalling ease. But the monastic perspective welcomes time as a gift from God, and seeks to put it to good use rather than allowing us to be used up by it… Liturgical time is essentially poetic time, oriented toward process rather than productivity, willing to wait attentively in stillness rather than always pushing to "get the job done."

BIBLICAL WISDOM

For everything there is a season, and a time for every matter under heaven: A time to be born, and a time to die; a time to plant, and a time to pluck what is planted, a time to kill, and a time to heal; a time to break down, and a time to build up; a time to weep, and a time to laugh; a time to mourn, and a time to dance; . . . a time to keep silence, and a time to speak. Ecclesiastes 3:1-4, 7b

SILENCE FOR MEDITATION

QUESTIONS TO PONDER

- What is our culture's primary "perspective on time"?
- Most of us live overloaded and overscheduled lives. What strategies might a community of faith use to help people get a new perspective on how to order their time?
- Reread Kathleen Norris's line about "liturgical time" again. In what ways might liturgical time be taken out of worship into daily life? How might that change our perspective on how to live meaningfully?

Psalm Fragment

I wait for the Lord, *my soul waits,*
And in his word I hope;
My soul waits for the Lord *more than watchmen for the morning,*
More than watchmen for the morning. Psalm 130:5-6

Journal Reflections

- The monastic mindset that Kathleen Norris portrays implies that rhythms are more essential than schedules. Write about the rhythms in your life. What are they? How do they nourish you and your spirituality?
- Write about the way schedules, appointments, objectives, demands, and deadlines harm the rhythms of your life. Are there things you might do to limit this harm and affirm the rhythms?
- Describe a time of waiting that resulted in a new awareness of God's presence in your life.

Prayers of Hope & Healing

Pray for people who are harried and driven, whose lives lack balance and harmony that they may learn to be still and know that God is God.

Prayer for Today

Lord of all eternity and all time, grant me patience to be still so that I may hear you speak to me through the sights, sounds, smells, feelings, and thoughts that surround me and fill me.

Notes

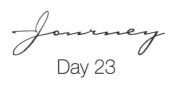
Day 23

WHEN IT (CELIBACY) WORKS, WHEN men have truly given up the idea of possessing women, healing can occur. I once met a woman in a monastery guest house who had come there because she was pulling herself together after being raped, and said she needed to feel safe around men again. I've seen young monks astonish an obese and homely college student by listening to her with as much interest and response as to her conventionally pretty roommate.

⁓

BIBLICAL WISDOM

Nevertheless, in the LORD woman is not independent of man or man independent of woman. For just as woman came from man, so man comes through woman; but all things come from God. 1 Corinthians 11:11-12

SILENCE FOR MEDITATION

QUESTIONS TO PONDER

- What do you think of Kathleen Norris's suggestion that celibacy is not just giving up sex, but giving up "the idea of possessing women"?
- Think of the images of women and girls and the treatment of women and girls in our society. What kind of healing do women and men and children need to experience?
- What are the assumptions and attitudes about women and girls in your faith community? Is there more that needs to be done to ensure the dignity, equality, and rights of women? Explain.

PSALM FRAGMENT

Young men and women alike,
*   old and young together!*
Let them praise the name of the LORD,
*   for his name alone is exalted;*
*   his glory is above earth and heaven.* Psalm 148:12-13

JOURNAL REFLECTIONS

- Write out a history of your formative experiences with the opposite sex from when you first became aware of your gender to the present moment. What does your history reveal about your present attitudes toward and assumptions about the opposite sex?
- Imagine that you had a chance to try living a celibate life with a group in a monastery. Would that be attractive to you? Why or why not? What might you say to a friend who asked you why you'd do such a thing?
- The monks in today's selection from Kathleen Norris acted in the belief that no one was beneath their interest and attention. How were they able to do that? Is that a personal quality that appeals to you? Why or why not?

PRAYERS OF HOPE & HEALING

Pray for those who are being or have been sexually abused or live in fear and shame because of their sexuality that they might experience the great worth God sees in them.

PRAYER FOR TODAY

Lord God, you have created us male and female in your image. Help me accept all people—myself included—as your equally beloved people.

NOTES

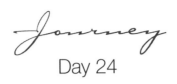
Day 24

As celibacy takes hold in a person...celibates become people who can radically affect those of us out "in the world." If only because they've learned how to listen without possessiveness, without imposing themselves. With someone who is practicing celibacy well, we may sense that we're being listened to in a refreshingly deep way. And this is the purpose of celibacy, not to attain some impossibly cerebral goal mistakenly conceived as "holiness" but to make oneself available to others, body and soul. Celibacy, simply put, is a form of ministry—not an achievement one can put on a resume but a subtle form of service to others.

Biblical Wisdom

Bear one another's burdens, and in this way you will fulfill the law of Christ.
Galatians 6:2

Silence for Meditation

Questions to Ponder

- In a culture that seems obsessed by sex and sexuality in what ways might celibacy be a countercultural corrective to the obsession?
- When people and relationships are over-sexualized, how might the practice of celibacy (permanently or temporarily) give people space to really be themselves and be open to who others really are?
- How might the practice of celibacy enable people "to listen without possessiveness, without imposing themselves"?

Psalm Fragment

"Come," my heart says, "seek his face!"
Your face, Lord, do I seek. Psalm 27:8

Journal Reflections

- Describe a time when you have felt truly welcomed and heard by another. What made that possible for you?
- Do you have any thoughts or feelings about sexuality and spirituality that you've never been able to discuss with anyone? Try writing about them in your journal.
- Do you agree with Kathleen Norris that celibacy might be "a form of ministry"? If so, how? If not, why not?

Prayers of Hope & Healing

Pray for all who have learned how to listen without possessiveness and without imposing themselves on others that their openness may be a path of healing.

Prayer for Today

Dear God, enable me to listen so others will speak and speak so that others may listen.

Notes

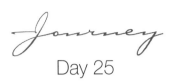

Day 25

MANY PEOPLE ARE JUST WAKING to the reality that unlimited expansion, what we call progress, is not possible in this world, and maybe looking to monks (who seek to live within limitations) as well as rural Dakotans (whose limitations are forced upon them by isolation and a harsh climate) can teach us how to live more realistically. These unlikely people might also help us overcome the pathological fear of death and the inability to deal with sickness and old age that plague American society. Consumerism is fed by a desire to forget our mortality.

BIBLICAL WISDOM

I have learned to be content with whatever I have. I know what it is to have little, and I know what it is to have plenty. In any and all circumstances I have learned the secret of being well-fed and of going hungry, of having plenty and of being in need. I can do all things through him who strengthens me. Philippians 4:11b-13

SILENCE FOR MEDITATION

QUESTIONS TO PONDER

- How does our culture react to the concept of limitations?
- Do you agree with Kathleen Norris that "consumerism is fed by a desire to forget our mortality"? Why or why not?
- What are the many ways in which "the pathological fear of death and the inability to deal with sickness and old age" are expressed in our society?

PSALM FRAGMENT

My soul is satisfied as with a rich feast,
*   and my mouth praises you with joyful lips*
*   when I think of you on my bed,*
*   and meditate on you in the watches of the night;*
*   for you have been my help...* Psalm 63:5-7a

JOURNAL REFLECTIONS

- We live in a consumerist society where we are always encouraged to buy more and more. How do you personally decide when enough is enough? Does your faith help you make that decision?
- Meditate in writing on your feelings about your eventual death. Do you live in acceptance or denial of your death? Explain.
- From your perspective, what would a realistically simple lifestyle look like? Is such a lifestyle attractive to you? Why or why not?

PRAYERS OF HOPE & HEALING

Pray for those who lack the basics they need to live a healthy and meaningful life that justice might prevail for them and their needs be met with dignity.

PRAYER FOR TODAY

Dear God, let me face my mortality with a healthy attitude and not cause harm to others in my futile attempts to deny it.

NOTES

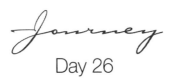

Day 26

I PARTAKE OF A CONTEMPLATIVE reality. Living close to such an expanse of land I find I have little incentive to move fast, little need for instant information. I have learned to trust the processes that take time, to value change that is not sudden or ill-considered but grows out of the ground of experience. Such change is properly defined as conversion, a word that at its root connotes not a change of essence, but of perspective, as turning around; turning back to or returning, turning one's attention.

⌒

BIBLICAL WISDOM

Let us test and examine our ways,
  and return to the LORD.
Let us lift up our hearts as well as our hands
  to God in heaven. Lamentations 3:40-41

SILENCE FOR MEDITATION

QUESTIONS TO PONDER

• What do you think Kathleen Norris means when she writes: "I partake of a contemplative reality"? Is that reality also accessible to people who live in cities and suburbs? If so, how? If not, why not?
• What are "the processes that take time"? Is there (and should there be) any room for such processes in our fast-moving society?
• Kathleen Norris learned to "value change that is not sudden or ill-considered but grows out of the ground of experience." How can such change be realized in a community of faith?

Psalm Fragments

Let me hear what God the Lord will speak,
for he will speak peace to his people,
to his faithful, to those who turn to him in their hearts. Psalm 85:8

Journal Reflections

- If conversion is understood as a change "of perspective, as turning around; turning back to or returning, turning one's attention," what experiences have you had that could be called *conversion experiences?*
- Have you experienced the "contemplative reality" which Kathleen Norris writes about? If so, what evokes the experience for you? If not, can you imagine having such an experience? What would it take?
- In your experience, in what ways does where one lives (in rural, urban or suburban areas) impact one's spiritual experience and awareness of God?

Prayers of Hope & Healing

Pray for people who want to change something about their lives but need the love and support of others to achieve their hopes.

Prayer for Today

Dear God, grant me this day the wisdom to know what to keep and what to release in my life.

Notes

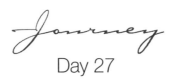
Day 27

I HAD WORRIED FOR A long time about what my religious conversion might do to my marriage. But I had held firm to the conviction that if the God of the gospels is real, and the commandment to love is primary, then my most intimate loving relationship would not be destroyed but enhanced by my faith. It had been a struggle, I said, and it took time, but my husband and I had worked things out. That question: "Why are you afraid?" was one that had been helpful, when I had remembered to ask it of myself during difficult times.

⁓

BIBLICAL WISDOM

Jesus looked at them and said, "For mortals it is impossible, but not for God; for God all things are possible." Peter began to say to him, "Look, we have left everything and followed you." Jesus said, "Truly I tell you, there is no one who has left house or brothers or sisters or mother or father or children or fields, for my sake and for the sake of the good news, who will not receive a hundredfold now in this age. Mark 10:27-30

SILENCE FOR MEDITATION

QUESTIONS TO PONDER

- Why do you think people are often willing to make great sacrifices for their Christian faith?
- What impact (positive and negative) might marriage have on a person's faith and what impact might a person's faith have on his or her marriage?
- In what ways do you think asking Kathleen Norris's question, "Why are you afraid?" might help people get through difficult times?

Psalm Fragment

God is our refuge and strength,
a very present help in trouble.
Therefore we will not fear, though the earth should change,
though the mountains shake in the heart of the sea;
though its waters roar and foam,
though the mountains tremble with its tumult. Psalm 46:1-3

Journal Reflections

- Reflect on your closest relationships. What connections do you see between your faith and those relationships?
- Have you ever had to risk losing or disappointing someone you care about because of your faith commitments? If so, write about how you handled it and what you learned. If not, write about how you imagine you would handle it.
- In difficult times, Kathleen Norris asks herself: "Why are you afraid?" Meditate on what questions you might ask yourself to give you a new perspective and see you through difficult times.

Prayers of Hope & Healing

Pray for those who suffer in their human relationships because of their trust in Christ that they may find strength and courage in faithfulness.

Prayer for Today

Gracious God, you have promised to be with me and sustain me when my life seems unmanageable. Grant me faith to cling to that promise.

Note

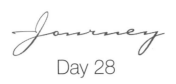

Day 28

I WAS BUILDING AN IMPRESSIVE storehouse of grievances, and I thought to myself, sleepily, *this could go on forever.* I sat upright, suddenly wide awake. Of course it could go on forever; that was exactly the point. I'd recently come upon the writings of a monk named Evagrius and realized that I had rapidly move beyond any justified frustration with my husband, and was becoming possessed by what Evagrius would have called the "bad thought" of anger… I got out my breviary and prayed the compline psalms 4 and 91, with their talk of peaceful sleep and angelic protection. Despite all I'd read in the desert monks about how prayer causes demons to flee, I was amazed to discover how quickly the anger dissipated. In its place, I found that what I was really feeling for my husband was fear…anger is the seed of compassion; I began to realize the truth of it.

ᔪ

BIBLICAL WISDOM

Put away from you all bitterness and wrath and anger and wrangling and slander, together with all malice, and be kind to one another, tenderhearted, forgiving one another, as God in Christ has forgiven you. Ephesians 4:31-32

SILENCE FOR MEDITATION

QUESTIONS TO PONDER

- In what ways is what Evagrius called the "bad thought" of anger nourished in our culture?
- How is anger handled in your family? Your faith community? Does it work, or are there possibly better ways to handle anger?
- Does it seem realistic that reading psalms can dissipate anger? Why or why not?

PSALM FRAGMENT

When you are disturbed, do not sin;
    ponder it on your beds, and be silent.
Offer right sacrifices,
    and put your trust in the LORD. Psalm 4:4-5

JOURNAL REFLECTIONS

- Do you have any spiritual practices (as Kathleen Norris does) to help you deal with anger or other unhelpful emotions? If so, describe how they work for you. If not, can you imagine spiritual practices that might help you deal with such feelings?
- Meditate in writing on the relationship between fear, anger, and love.
- Have you ever used a breviary or daily office as a form of prayer? If so, describe the experience. If not, why not give it a try?

PRAYERS OF HOPE & HEALING

Pray for those who are consumed by anger, bitterness, fear, and any other unhelpful emotion that their inner turmoil might be dissolved in the love of God and peace of Christ.

PRAYER FOR TODAY

Dear God, help me find safe ways to express my anger and courage to set it aside when it no longer serves any useful purpose.

NOTES

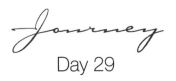

Day 29

ALL OF US, I SUSPECT, have times when we're made to suffer simply for being who and what we are, and we become adept at inventing means of escape. But Jeremiah reminded me that the pain that comes from one's identity, that grows out of the response to a call, can't be escaped or pushed aside. It must be gone through. He led me into the heart of pain, forcing me to recognize that to answer a call as a prophet, or a poet for that matter, is to reject the authority of credentials, of human valuation of any kind, accepting only the authority of the call itself. It was as a writer that Jeremiah spoke to me, and it was as a writer I listened. I couldn't have asked for a better companion.

BIBLICAL WISDOM

Now the word of the LORD came to me saying, "Before I formed you in the womb I knew you, and before you were born I consecrated you; I appointed you a prophet to the nations." Then I said, "Ah, Lord GOD! Truly I do not know how to speak, for I am only a boy." But the LORD said to me, "Do not say, 'I am only a boy'; for you shall go to all to whom I send you, and you shall speak whatever I command you. Do not be afraid of them, for I am with you to deliver you, says the LORD." Jeremiah 1:4-8

SILENCE FOR MEDITATION

QUESTIONS TO PONDER

- How does our culture react to people who "reject the authority of credentials, of human valuation of any kind…"?
- How does your faith community react to those who "reject the authority of credentials, of human valuation of any kind, accepting only the authority of the call itself"? Are there ways to discern the validity of a prophet's or poet's call?
- Who are the prophets and poets in your community? How is their message received— or not received?

PSALM FRAGMENT

It is for your sake that I have borne reproach,
*   that shame has covered my face.*
I have become a stranger to my kindred,
*   an alien to my mother's children.* Psalm 69:7-8

JOURNAL REFLECTIONS

- Have you ever suffered "simply for being who and what [you] are..."? If so, describe the feelings and your response. If not, can you imagine what it would be like?
- Do you feel that God is calling you in any way? If so, describe the call and how you are responding? If not, can you imagine beginning a process of discerning where God might be leading you? How would you begin? Who could you talk with?
- Have you ever experienced "the pain that comes from one's identity, that grows out of the response to a call..."? If so, describe the pain and how you lived (or are living) through it. If not, what resources would you have for living through such pain should you ever experience it?

PRAYERS OF HOPE & HEALING

Pray for all who are struggling to discern and accept their call that they may have clarity and courage in the process despite any obstacles.

PRAYER FOR TODAY

Dear God, when you call let me hear and answer with trust and courage.

NOTES

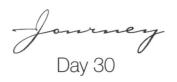
Day 30

As a scholar Peter Brown has written in a study of the era (of the desert fathers) entitled *The Making of Late Antiquity*, what the monks meant by demonic was "an extension of the self." They spoke often of being tested by demons but, as Brown writes, these trials "meant passing through a stage in the growth of awareness of the lower frontiers of the personality." The psychological insight of the monks is often strikingly modern. When a monk asked the eminently sane Abba Poemen, "How do the demons fight against me?" Poemen replied that the demons do not fight us at all, as long as we are doing our own will. It is only when we begin to resist and question ourselves, seeking another, better way of life that the struggles begin. "Our own wills become the demons, and it is these which attack us."

~

Biblical Wisdom

I can will what is right, but I cannot do it. For I do not do the good I want, but the evil I do not want is what I do. Now if I do what I do not want, it is no longer I that do it, but sin that dwells within me. So I find it to be a law that when I want to do what is good, evil lies close at hand. Romans 7:18b-21

Silence for Meditation

Questions to Ponder

- In what ways might it (or might it not) be helpful to think of the "demonic" as "an extension of the self"?
- Given Kathleen Norris's understanding of the "demonic," in what ways might institutions, for example, the church, be "tested by demons." How should such testing be met?
- To use Peter Brown's phrase, what are the "the lower frontiers of the personality"? How do we become aware of them, and what might be the consequences of such "awareness"?

Psalm Fragment

Teach me to do your will,
for you are my God.
Let your good spirit lead me
on a level path. Psalm 143:10

Journal Reflections

- Abba Poemen said, "Our own wills become the demons, and it is these which attack us." Does this resonate with your experience? Explain.
- Reflect on today's *Biblical Wisdom* and then journal about some things you wanted to do but didn't and some things you didn't want to do but did. Where is God in these experiences?
- When you find your conscience struggling with your will, what biblical, spiritual, and relational resources do you have to help you in the struggle?

Prayers of Hope & Healing

Pray for those who are trying to give up old, unhealthy habits or pick up new, life-enhancing habits that they may find the strength to resist the temptation to give up.

Prayer for Today

God of all hopefulness, help me stick to my spiritual growth disciplines even when it seems pointless and futile.

Notes

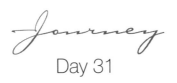

Day 31

CONVERTING A PAINFUL INHERITANCE INTO something good requires all the discernment we can muster, both from what is within us, and what we can glean from mentors. The worst of the curses that people inflict on us, the real abuse and terror, can't be forgotten or undone, but they can be put to good use in the new life that one has taken up. It is a kind of death; the lid closes on what went before. But the past is not denied. And we are still here, with all of our talents, gifts, and failings, our strengths and weaknesses. All the baggage comes along; nothing wasted, nothing lost. Perhaps the greatest blessing that religious inheritance can bestow is an open mind, one that can listen without judging. It is rare enough that we recognize it in another when we encounter it. I often see it in people who have attained what the monastic tradition terms "detachment," an ability to live at peace with the reality of whatever happens. Such people do not have a closed-off air, nor a boastful demeanor. In them, it is clear, their wounds have opened the way to compassion for others. And compassion is the strength and soul of a religion.

⌒

BIBLICAL WISDOM

We also boast in our sufferings, knowing that suffering produces endurance, and endurance produces character, and character produces hope, and hope does not disappoint us, because God's love has been poured into our hearts through the Holy Spirit that has been given to us. Romans 5:3-5

SILENCE FOR MEDITATION

QUESTIONS TO PONDER

• What does it mean for an individual or community to take up "a new life" in the wake of the experience of "real abuse and terror"?

- What does your community do to help people who have been traumatized by abuse, addiction, or other tragedies? Could more be done?
- Name the "wounded healers" in your faith community—people who have suffered greatly and then used that experience to help others.

PSALM FRAGMENT

Will you not revive us again,
*   so that your people may rejoice in you?*
Show us your steadfast love, O LORD,
*   and grant us your salvation.*
Let me hear what God the LORD will speak,
*   for he will speak peace to his people,*
*   to his faithful, to those who turn to him in their hearts.* Psalm 85:6-8

JOURNAL REFLECTIONS

- Has your life given you a "painful inheritance"? If so, describe the experience. What (and who) has helped you to take up a "new life" in spite of it? If not, reflect on people you know who have had a "painful inheritance." What helped them to cope and move on?
- Reflect on your life experience. What are the "talents, gifts, and failings… strengths and weaknesses" that you can bring to "converting a painful inheritance into something good"?
- Have you experienced the "detachment," the "ability to live at peace with the reality of whatever happens," of which Kathleen Norris writes? If so, how did you get there? If not, how might you get there?

PRAYERS OF HOPE & HEALING

Pray for those who suffer from abuse, addiction, or abandonment that they may be led to safe places, caring communities, healing helpers, and a new and good life.

PRAYER FOR TODAY

Dear God, through your transforming Spirit let my bad experiences be converted into something good.

NOTES

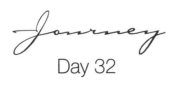

Day 32

DURING THAT TIME I BECAME a writer. I used to think that writing had substituted for religion in my life, but I've come to see that it has acted as a spiritual discipline, giving me the tools I needed to rediscover my religious heritage. It is my Christian inheritance that largely defines me, but for years I didn't know that.

❧

BIBLICAL WISDOM

For I the Lord your God am a jealous God, visiting the iniquity of the fathers upon the children to the third and the fourth generation of those who hate me, but showing steadfast love to thousands of those who love me and keep my command-ments. Exodus 20: 5b-6

SILENCE FOR MEDITATION

QUESTIONS TO PONDER

- How does your community welcome those who have been missing in action for months or years when they come back?
- Many people experience "dry" spells in their faith journey. In what ways does your faith community acknowledge the experience and encourage people who are going through it?
- What exactly is a "Christian inheritance"? How can it be accessed by peo-ple who have fallen away from faith and the community of faith?

PSALM FRAGMENT

As a deer longs for flowing streams,
*   so my soul longs for you, O God.*
My soul thirsts for God,
*   for the living God.*
When shall I come and behold
*   the face of God?* Psalm 42:1-2

Journal Reflections

- What is your "Christian inheritance"? Where did it come from and how does it "define" you?
- Do you have any activities that could be seen as having "substituted for religion" in your life? If so, what are they and could they become a "spiritual discipline," helping you rediscover your religious heritage?
- Who in your experience has most influenced the faith you have today? Write about that influence and then wonder in your journal who you are influencing in matters of faith.

Prayers of Hope & Healing

Pray for people of faith that they may be careful when adding to the religious inheritance of others.

Prayer for Today

God of all faithfulness, help me to mine the treasures of my religious inheritance and use it as a tool for continued growth.

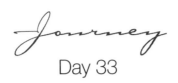

Day 33

"WHAT IS SIN?" IT NEVER occurred to me to go to a church for the answer. If the church hadn't taught me in my first twenty years what sin was, it probably never would. I now realize that the question was raised by the pious Protestant grandmother at my core. I had no idea she was there, and didn't know how to listen to her. I didn't realize it at the time, but my move in 1974 from New York to South Dakota was an attempt to hear her voice more clearly. It was a search for inheritance, for place. It was also a religious pilgrimage; on the ground of my grandmother's faith I would find both the means and the end of my search.

⌐

BIBLICAL WISDOM

My child, if you accept my words
and treasure up my commandments within you,
making your ear attentive to wisdom
and inclining your heart to understanding;
if you indeed cry out for insight,
and raise your voice for understanding...
then you will understand the fear of the LORD
and find the knowledge of God. Proverbs 2:1-5

SILENCE FOR MEDITATION

QUESTIONS TO PONDER

- What does it mean to "search for inheritance, for place"?
- How can a faith community help people in their "search for inheritance, for place"?
- In what ways might her "grandmother's faith" be "both the means and the end of [Kathleen Norris's] search" for inheritance and place?

Psalm Fragment

How can young people keep their way pure?
By guarding it according to your word.
With my whole heart I seek you;
*   do not let me stray from your commandments.*
I treasure your word in my heart,
*   so that I may not sin against you.* Psalm 119:9-11

Journal Reflections

- Have you found your "inheritance and place"? Explain.
- Where do you go with your faith questions? Who do you ask? Why?
- How would you go about answering Kathleen Norris's question, "What is sin?"

Prayers of Hope & Healing

Pray for all who are looking for their "inheritance and place" that they may finally come to the place where they are at home.

Prayer for Today

Loving God, let me receive and live out of my inheritance and find comfort and joy in the places you have prepared for me.

Notes

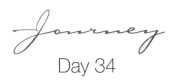

Day 34

GREGORY OF NYSSA, A FOURTH-CENTURY theologian, [said] that sin is the failure to grow. In our own century, Carl Jung has reminded us that to grow we must eventually stop running from our "shadow" and turn to face it.

~

BIBLICAL WISDOM

If we say that we have no sin, we deceive ourselves, and the truth is not in us. If we confess our sins, he who is faithful and just will forgive us our sins and cleanse us from all unrighteousness. 1 John 3:8-9

SILENCE FOR MEDITATION

QUESTIONS TO PONDER

- In what ways is the "failure to grow" rightly understood as sin?
- What does it mean to say that in order to grow we must "stop running from our 'shadow' and turn to face it"?
- In what ways might awareness of God's forgiveness of our "failure to grow" empower us to "stop running from our 'shadow'" and begin to grow?

PSALM FRAGMENT

Then I acknowledged my sin to you,
  and I did not hide my iniquity;
I said, "I will confess my transgressions to the LORD,"
  and you forgave the guilt of my sin. Psalm 32:5

JOURNAL REFLECTIONS

- Meditate on sin as the "failure to grow." What kind of growth do you think Kathleen Norris is writing about? Does this understanding of sin resonate with you?

- Meditate on your life. Where are you growing? What are the reasons for your growth? Where are you failing to grow? What are the reasons for your failure?
- Spiritually speaking, what "growth" strategies could strengthen you or could you adopt to overcome obstacles to growth in your life?

PRAYERS OF HOPE & HEALING

Pray for those who face their shadow and commit to growth that they may find hope and joy in the unfolding of their lives.

PRAYER FOR TODAY

Gracious God, my Creator, grant me grace to accept my faults and limitations so that I can more fully embrace the gifts and opportunities you set before me.

NOTES

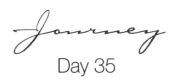

Day 35

AT FIFTEEN ...I HAD BEEN visited by the noonday demon and, in ways I was not to become fully aware of for many years, my life was changed forever. The fear of the daily had intruded into my consciousness at a time when it could do real harm. A shy, pudgy teenager, suffering from the loneliness that so many teenagers feel, I had just become more lonely. My fearful thoughts of the future seemed so absurd I could not speak of them to anyone.

BIBLICAL WISDOM

So let us not grow weary in doing what is right, for we will reap at harvest time, if we do not give up. So then, whenever we have an opportunity, let us work for the good of all... Galatians 6:9-10

SILENCE FOR MEDITATION

QUESTIONS TO PONDER

- The "noonday demon" is a metaphor for the depression and boredom we may feel with the daily round of activities that make up our lives and provide the raw materials for growth. It is the inducement to abandon the struggle to be faithful to God's call to growth. What evidence is there that the "noonday demon" is alive and well in our culture?
- What resources might the community of faith have for helping people resist the "noonday demon"?
- How might a faith community help people to experience God rather than meaninglessness in the quotidian or ordinary activities and duties of daily life?

PSALM FRAGMENT

How long, O LORD? Will you forget me forever?
How long will you hide your face from me?
How long must I bear pain in my soul,
and have sorrow in my heart all day long? Psalm 13:1-2

JOURNAL REFLECTIONS

- Meditate on your life. Have you ever met the "noonday demon"? If so, describe the experience in writing. What, if any, spiritual practices were available to you to send the demon away? If not, can you imagine how you might respond should the "noonday demon" come calling?
- Remember your childhood. What experiences (both positive and negative) continue to shape your approach to life? What might you do to enhance the impact of the positive and diminish the impact of the negative?
- Do you relate to the future with fear or hope? Explain. If fear, what is the source of your fear? If hope, what is the ground of your hope?

PRAYERS OF HOPE & HEALING

Pray for those from whom the "noonday demon" steals the joy in simple, commonplace, ordinary things that they may see that every ordinary thing and every ordinary person is a doorway to God.

PRAYER FOR TODAY

God of all delight, help me to turn my back on the "noonday demon" and find you—and joy—in ordinary things.

NOTES

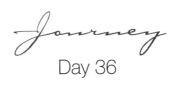

Day 36

TO MAKE THE POEM OF our faith, we must learn not to settle for a false certitude but to embrace ambiguity and mystery. Our goal will be to recover our original freedom, our childlike (but never childish) wisdom. It will be difficult to lose our adult self-consciousness (here the discipline of writing can help us), difficult not to confuse our worship with self-expression. (All too often the call for "creativity" in worship simply leads to bad art.) We will need a powerful catalyst. In any institution, while there's always the sacred "way we've always done it," and certainly a place for the traditions that such an attitude reflects, there is also a spirit at work that has more to do with being than with doing.

⁓

BIBLICAL WISDOM

Truly I tell you, whoever does not receive the kingdom of God as a little child will never enter it. Mark 10:15

SILENCE FOR MEDITATION

QUESTIONS TO PONDER

- What do you think Kathleen Norris means when she writes: "To make the poem of our faith, we must learn not to settle for a false certitude but to embrace ambiguity and mystery"?
- How would you describe the distinction between "being" and "doing"? Which do you value most and why?
- How are "traditions" and "creativity" balanced in your faith community?

PSALM FRAGMENT

Praise the LORD with the lyre;
  make melody to him with the harp of ten strings.
Sing to him a new song;
  play skillfully on the strings, with loud shouts. Psalm 33:2-3

Journal Reflections

- Begin in your journal to write "the poem of [your] faith." It is a poem you will continue to write for the rest of your life. Read it, edit it, add to it regularly.
- Has the "discipline of writing" in your journal helped you at all "to lose [your] adult self-consciousness"? Explain.
- Meditate on your life. Are you open to and comfortable with "ambiguity and mystery"? Explain.

Prayers of Hope & Healing

Pray for worship leaders that they may find balance between keeping old, familiar traditions and introducing new and innovative ideas in public worship that help people write the poem of their faith.

Prayer for Today

God of all eternity, help me be open to new ways, new people, and new traditions, and help me be open to mystery as I write the poem of my faith.

Notes

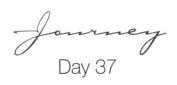

Day 37

THE DAKOTAS HAVE ALWAYS BEEN a place to be *from:* some 80 percent of homesteaders left within the first twenty years of settlement, and our boom-and-bust agricultural and oil industry economy has kept people moving in and out (mostly out) ever since. Many small-town schools and pulpits operate with revolving doors, adding to the instability.

BIBLICAL WISDOM

So Abram went, as the LORD had told him; and Lot went with him. Abram was seventy-five years old when he departed from Haran. Abram took his wife Sarai and his brother's son Lot, and all the possessions that they had gathered, and the persons whom they had acquired in Haran; and they set forth to go to the land of Canaan. Genesis 12:4-5

SILENCE FOR MEDITATION

QUESTIONS TO PONDER

- How do the comings and goings of people impact both your faith community and the larger community in which you live?
- Does your faith community have strategies and programs to help people who are either moving away from or into your community? If so, what are they and how effective are they? If not, what might be done?
- Where do you think God might be found in the experience of people and communities in transition?

PSALM FRAGMENT

By the waters of Babylon—
there we sat down and there we wept
when we remembered Zion. Psalm 137:1-3

Journal Reflections

- How often has your family moved? What values underscored decisions to move or not to move?
- How have you seen God at work through the places you have chosen to go and the places you have chosen to stay?
- Have you ever experienced a sense of homesickness for a place you used to be? Explore in writing both the losses and gains of moving.

Prayers of Hope & Healing

Pray for all who are forced to move from their homes because of economic hardships, natural disasters, or because of political unrest and war that they may be sustained in their loss, comforted in their grief, and find a new and safe community. Pray for all who move to follow new opportunities and the hope for a better life that they may find that better life in their new community.

Prayer for Today

Thank you for all the communities that been a part of my life and the people in them who have helped shape who I am today.

Notes

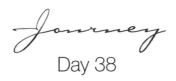

Day 38

To some extent, wariness about change is a kind of prairie wisdom. The word's origins lie in the marketplace, as in "exchange," and negative connotations abound, like "to shortchange" or deceive. But the sad truth is that the harder we resist change, and the more we resent anyone who demands change of us, the more we shortchange ourselves. Who could be more impoverished than the man who, in hearing news of a former teacher, exclaimed in a tavern, "That old cow? She used to make me read. Said I couldn't graduate till I read all she wanted. Well, I showed her; I haven't read a book since."

⌐

BIBLICAL WISDOM

And the one who was seated on the throne said, "See, I am making all things new." Also he said, "Write this, for these words are trustworthy and true." Revelations 21:5

SILENCE FOR MEDITATION

QUESTIONS TO PONDER

- Do you agree with Kathleen Norris that "the harder we resist change, and the more we resent anyone who demands change of us, the more we shortchange ourselves"? Why or why not?
- Does your community of faith embrace or resist change? If change is embraced, what motivates people to accept it? If change is resisted, what motivates people to reject it?
- What strategies might a community of faith employ to successfully negotiate change?

Psalm Fragment

Create in me a clean heart, O God,
*   and put a new and right spirit within me.*
Do not cast me away from your presence,
*   and do not take your holy spirit from me.*
Restore to me the joy of your salvation,
*   and sustain in me a willing spirit.* Psalm 51:10-12

Journal Reflections

- How do you deal with change in your life? In your relationships? In institutions you are a part of?
- In what, if any, ways does your faith and spiritual practice help you negotiate change?
- In your life, how do you discern when change is good and necessary (even if difficult) and when change is something to be wary of?

Prayers of Hope & Healing

Pray for those faced with tumultuous change that they may have the wisdom to say yes when yes is called for and no when no is called for.

Prayer for Today

God of eternity who does not change, help me change what needs to change in my life and preserve what needs to be preserved.

Notes

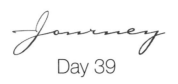

Day 39

IT IS THE COMMUNITY THAT suffers when it refuses to validate any outside standards, and won't allow even the legitimate exercise of authority by the professionals it has hired. . . Pastors are expected to attend women's Bible study meetings, but sometimes are resented when they make comments designed to stimulate discussion, as the women are used to simply reading aloud the printed lessons.

BIBLICAL WISDOM

Whenever you enter a town and its people welcome you, eat what is set before you; cure the sick who are there, and say to them, "The kingdom of God has come near to you." But whenever you enter a town and they do not welcome you, go out into its streets and say, "Even the dust of your town that clings to our feet, we wipe off in protest against you. Yet know this: the kingdom of God has come near." Luke 10:8-12

SILENCE FOR MEDITATION

QUESTIONS TO PONDER

- What does our culture teach about welcoming the stranger?
- How are newcomers welcomed into your neighborhood? Your faith community?
- Why do we often feel suspicious of and threatened by strangers? What might we do to overcome these feelings?

PSALM FRAGMENT

May there be abundance of grain in the land;
*   may it wave on the tops of the mountains;*
*   may its fruit be like Lebanon;*
*   and may people blossom in the cities*
*   like the grass of the field.* Psalm 72:16

Journal Reflections

- Reflect on your past experience. Describe a time when you felt really unwelcome? What caused you to feel that way? How did you respond?
- Make a list of people who count as friends today who were once total strangers to you. Write about how together you moved from being strangers to being friends.
- Have you ever felt like you brought gifts to a community that were not appreciated and used? If so, write about the experience. If not, imagine what it would be like to have such an experience.

Prayers of Hope & Healing

Pray for people who are moving to new and unfamiliar places that they may be warmly welcomed as valuable members of their new community. Pray also for those who feel friendless and unappreciated that others may recognize and rejoice in their true worth.

Prayer for Today

God of hospitality, lead me to people who need a word of welcome and give me courage to speak to them.

Notes

Day 40

WE MAKE SUCH A FUSS about "seeking God." We're anxious about so many things, and faith, prayer, and searching for God are not accepted. Are we doing it right? Will a retreat teach us a better way? Which method of prayer will be most effective for us? What church congregation will best "feed us spiritually"? Probably the best thing we can do is to relax, take a deep breath, stop thinking about what we want or need, and forget about it. Seeking God, that is. Instead we might wait, and begin to silently ponder the ways in which God may already have been seeking us, all along, in the faulty, scary stuff of our ordinary lives.

⌒

BIBLICAL WISDOM

For thus says the LORD GOD: I myself will search for my sheep, and will seek them out. As shepherds seek out their flocks when they are among their scattered sheep, so I will seek out my sheep. I will rescue them from all the places to which they have been scattered on a day of clouds and thick darkness. Ezekiel 34:11-12

SILENCE FOR MEDITATION

QUESTIONS TO PONDER

- What might be wrong about making "such a fuss about 'seeking God'"?
- How might spiritual disciplines help you in opening up to the awareness and experience of God? How might spiritual disciplines actually hinder you in opening up to God?
- How can the members of a faith community help each other to discover "the ways in which God may already have been seeking us, all along, in the faulty, scary stuff of our ordinary lives"?

PSALM FRAGMENT

The LORD is my shepherd, I shall not want.
He makes me lie down in green pastures;
  he leads me beside still waters;
  he restores my soul.
He leads me in right paths
  for his name's sake. Psalm 23:1-3

JOURNAL REFLECTIONS

- Are you anxious about "faith, prayer, and searching for God"? If so, describe your anxiety. What might you do to relieve the anxiety? If not, write about how you feel about your faith, prayer, and search for God.
- Reflect on the spiritual disciplines you practice. Do they feel as if they are helping or hindering your openness to God's presence in your life? Explain.
- Meditate in writing on what it might be like "to relax, take a deep breath, stop thinking about what [you] want or need, and forget about it. Seeking God, that is," and simply trust that God is seeking you?

PRAYERS OF HOPE & HEALING

Pray for those on a spiritual journey that they would learn to relax into God, to rest in God's mercy, and to wait in the silence where God is known in love.

PRAYER FOR TODAY

Dear Lord and Shepherd, thank you for seeking me and providing for me all that I truly need. Grant me the confidence to trust that you always will.

NOTES

JOURNEY'S END

You have finished your *40-Day Journey with Kathleen Norris*. I hope it has been a good journey and that along the way you have learned much, experienced much, and found good resources to deepen your faith and practice. As a result of this journey:

- How are you different?
- What have you learned?
- What have you experienced?
- In what ways has your faith and practice been transformed?

NOTES

Do you want to continue the journey? If you would, there is a list of Kathleen Norris's books on the next page that will help you delve further into the thought, experience, and practice of this remarkable woman.

For Further Reading

Amazing Grace: A Vocabulary of Faith. New York: Riverhead, 1999.

Dakota: A Spiritual Geography. New York: Mariner, 2001.

The Journey: New and Selected Poems, 1969-1999. Pittsburg: Pittsburg University Press, 2001

The Cloister Walk. New York: Riverhead, 1996.

The Quotidian Mysteries: Laundry, Liturgy, and "Women's Work." Mahwah: Paulist, 1998.

The Virgin of Bennington. New York: Riverhead, 2002.

Sources

Day 1: *The Cloister Walk*, 251-52

Day 2: *Amazing Grace*, 63

Day 3: *Dakota: A Spiritual Geography*, 18

Day 4: *Dakota: A Spiritual Geography*, 116

Day 5: *Dakota: A Spiritual Geography*, 129

Day 6: *The Cloister Walk*, 340

Day 7: *Amazing Grace*, 44

Day 8: *Amazing Grace*, 20

Day 9: *Amazing Grace*, 55

Day 10: *Dakota: A Spiritual Geography*, 95

Day 11: *Amazing Grace*, 324-25

Day 12: *Amazing Grace*, 17

Day 13: *The Cloister Walk*, 33-34

Day 14: *The Cloister Walk*, 59

Day 15: *Amazing Grace*, 58

Day 16: *The Cloister Walk*, 93

Day 17: *The Cloister Walk*, 97

Day 18: *The Cloister Walk*, 100-101

Day 19: *Amazing Grace*, 69

Day 20: *Amazing Grace*, 316-17

Day 21: *Amazing Grace*, 318

Day 22: *The Cloister Walk*, xix

Day 23: *The Cloister Walk*, 120

Day 24: *The Cloister Walk*, 121

Day 25: *Dakota: A Spiritual Geography*, 120

Day 26: *Dakota: A Spiritual Geography*, 145-46

Day 27: *Amazing Grace*, 304

Day 28: *The Cloister Walk*, 138

Day 29: *The Cloister Walk*, 38

Day 30: *Amazing Grace*, 46

Day 31: *Amazing Grace*, 29

Day 32: *Dakota: A Spiritual Geography*, 92

Day 33: *Dakota: A Spiritual Geography*, 93

Day 34: *Dakota: A Spiritual Geography*, 99

Day 35: *The Cloister Walk*, 132

Day 36: *The Cloister Walk*, 62

Day 37: *Dakota: A Spiritual Geography*, 8

Day 38: *Dakota: A Spiritual Geography*, 51

Day 39: *Dakota: A Spiritual Geography*, 60

Day 40: *Amazing Grace*, 299

We gratefully acknowledge the publishers who granted permission to reprint material from the following sources:

Excerpts from *Dakota:* A spiritual Geography by Kathleen Norris. Copyright © 1993 by Kathleen Norris. Reprinted by permission of Houghton Mifflin Company. All rights reserved.

Excerpts from *Amazing Grace:* A Vocabulary of Faith by Kathleen Norris. Copyright © 1998 by Kathleen Norris. Reprinted by permission of Riverhead Books, a division of Penguin Books USA Inc.

Excerpts from *The Cloister Walk* by Kathleen Norris. Copyright © 1996 by Kathleen Norris. Reprinted by permission of Riverhead Books, a division of Penguin Books USA Inc.

NOTES

NOTES

Notes

NOTES

NOTES